Modern

JENNY McCOY

Photography by Pernille Loof

Éclairs

And OTHER SWEET AND SAVORY PUFFS

HOUGHTON MIFFLIN HARCOURT

Boston • New York • 2016

Prop styling by Brian Heiser
Food styling by Junita Bognanni
Recipe testing by Joanne Allegra and Carly DeFilippo

For information about permission to reproduce selections from this
book, write to trade.permissions@hmhco.com or to Permissions,
Houghton Mifflin Harcourt Publishing Company, 3 Park Avenue,
19th Floor, New York, New York 10016.

www.hmhco.com

Library of Congress Cataloging-in-Publication Data
McCoy, Jenny.
    Modern éclairs : and other sweet and savory puffs / Jenny McCoy ;
Photography by Pernille Loof.
        pages cm
    Includes index.
    ISBN 978-0-544-55719-2 (paper over board); 978-0-544-55826-7 (ebook)
    1. Pastry. 2. Desserts I. Title
    TX773.M165 2016
    641.86'5—dc23
                        2015019994

Design by Rachel Newborn

Printed in China
C&C 10 9 8 7 6 5 4 3 2 1

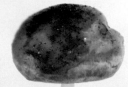

To *mes petits choux*,
Ellis and Simon

Contents

Foreword

In the wild world of dessert, there is always a pastry that intrigues and inspires. Where possibilities are endless and imagination runs rampant. Éclairs are just that. The flavors! The fillings! The size! The shape! The textures! They're modern, hip, and forever exciting. It's no surprise that Jenny's obsession with them has led to this sweet and savory pastry adventure ahead.

I don't believe I've ever met anyone who knows how to balance the fun and sweet side of life with the skill of a trained pastry chef quite like Jenny. She has an amazing drive and passion that is like no other, and it comes through in everything she does, especially her food. Jenny worked her way up through the highest acclaimed restaurants, so it's no wonder she's a star. She is clever and creative, but honors simplicity through the classics like the pro that she is. Anything and everything that she dreams up is as such—remarkably simple, yet refined and utterly delicious.

Christina Tosi
Chef and founder, Momofuku Milk Bar

Introduction

OH, PÂTE À CHOUX, IT'S FINALLY YOUR TURN FOR THE LIMELIGHT

Move over, macarons and meringue . . . it's time for another classic French sweet to get a makeover. And this time, we are not only going sweet, but we are going savory, too.

Did you know that *pâte à choux* literally translates to "paste of cabbage"? Doesn't that sound delicious? Are you beginning to wonder if this book is about cabbage cookery? Of course not! This cookbook is the exploration of pâte à choux, a glorious dough that, when baked, puffs into a shape that sort of resembles a head of cabbage. (Hence the reason for the name, which, by the way, really means a pastry that puffs—as in cream puffs, éclairs, profiteroles, and so forth.)

To make pâte à choux, all you need are seven staple baking ingredients: water, milk, butter, salt, sugar, bread flour, and eggs. With just a few basic tools—a saucepan and a rubber spatula—you can whip up a batch of the dough. Armed with a pastry bag and a few piping tips, you can create a variety of shapes. Pop them in the oven, and voilà! You have puffed delights that can be filled and adorned with any flavor combination you can think up.

Pâte à choux is truly amazing. In my humble opinion, it is unparalleled in both ease of preparation and versatility. How many types of pastry dough can be used for both sweet *and* savory recipes? How many types of pastry dough can be piped into *any* shape imaginable? Not many. So get ready to have some fun without much fuss!

WHAT'S SO MODERN ABOUT PÂTE À CHOUX, ANYWAY?

Throughout my career as a professional pastry chef, my specialty has been taking the tried and true, the traditional, the terribly typical, and making them better. Tweaking a base recipe to my perfection, then exploring how to use that recipe in a variety of ways, is my forte. This book is my love letter to pâte à choux. Its recipes will inspire you to make all sorts of new and delicious sweets and savories and give you the tools to create new flavor combinations of your own.

Most recipes for pâte à choux are fairly similar, with a minor twist here and there—some call for a combination of milk and water, some use just water, and some use instant dry milk. Some require all-purpose flour and some require bread flour. Some are baked at a very high temperature, and some at a low temperature. It's not my pâte à choux recipe that is especially modern. What is modern is how I've used it throughout the book to create imaginative baked goods that you will not find in your local bakery case.

WHAT THE PUFF IS IN THIS COOKBOOK?

In the beginning, I will teach you the technique for making pâte à choux. Although I've made the recipe very simple, be sure to read it through entirely before you get started. Mastering this one easy recipe will ensure your success when making recipes throughout the rest of the book.

It would have been unthinkable to write a book on pâte à choux without a generous nod to the traditional pastries it's known for. So in the next chapter, you will learn how to make the most celebrated recipes for pâte à choux, such as Cream Puffs filled with whipped cream (page 45), Chantilly Swans (page 50), and Classic Profiteroles with vanilla bean ice cream and chocolate sauce (page 57). You will also learn a few twists on the classics, like a colorful take on a traditional croquembouche (page 76), the exquisite French dessert often served at weddings.

As for the next four chapters—Fruity, Chocolate, Frozen, and Holiday—you will find recipes for modern interpretations such as Fruity Pâte à Choux Pops (page 91), Mississippi Mud Puffs (page 149), Banana Split Éclairs (page 194), and coconut-dusted Snowflakes (page 237).

In the final chapter—Savory—we will go way beyond the typical sweet application of pâte à choux. I will teach you new and exciting ways to use pâte à choux for scrumptious salty recipes. Yes, we've all heard of gougères (a.k.a. cheese puffs), but have you ever made a lobster roll in an éclair shell, or a BLT in a cream puff shell? I didn't think so. I hope now you will.

THE BRIEFEST HISTORY OF PÂTE À CHOUX (AS I KNOW IT)

According to legend (and some seriously dusty cookbooks), pâte à choux was invented by Catherine de' Medici's famous chef, Pantanelli (spelled various ways, depending on the source), in 1540 or so. There are two possibilities:

1) Pantanelli invented a pastry that could be made quickly while traveling at the request of his employer. (Remember: Catherine was forced to leave Florence . . . and thankfully, she had the good sense to bring along her chef while on the run.)

2) Pantanelli was a culinary genius who, upon Catherine's marriage to the Duke of Orléans (who later became the King of France, Henry II), decided to make a gâteau with a newly invented dough, *pâte à Pantanelli*, for the king.

The dough changed names as it changed hands over the centuries, and was used in many applications, mostly those similar to popovers. But it didn't reach its full potential until finally being perfected and published in 1815 by the great French chef Marie-Antoine Carême, in his famous cookbook *Le Pâtissier royal parisien*. Carême's version of the dough recipe is what is now most commonly used when making profiteroles, cream puffs, and éclairs.

And the rest is history. . . .

LET'S GET A LITTLE NERDY. JUST A LITTLE.

Pâte à choux dough is different from many other baked types of dough because it doesn't require a chemical leavening agent, such as baking soda or baking powder.

Pâte à choux dough uses the simple magic of heat and *a lot* of moisture to create steam. Mixing the dough vigorously strengthens the gluten in the bread flour. The steam trapped in the strong gluten molecules is what creates large pockets in the dough. The pockets are what cause the pâte à choux to have a hollow interior and rise to its glorious heights.

Pretty cool, huh?

GET CREATIVE! PRETTY, PRETTY PLEASE . . .

This book is about having fun! I encourage you to use your imagination to make a pastry that combines a different filling or glaze than I've directed. For example, if a pistachio Paris-Brest, using Pistachio Pastry Cream (page 116) for the filling, sounds delicious to you, go for it! Or, if you want to swap out the Lemon Curd (page 112) for Bittersweet Chocolate Mousse (page 132) to make chocolate cream pie éclairs instead of lemon meringue, I see no reason to stop you.

Ingredients

MMM . . .
IT'S TIME FOR THE GOOD STUFF

Bread Flour and All-Purpose Flour:

I recommend King Arthur brand unbleached flours. They are a bit more expensive than other brands, but well worth the investment because they are a very consistent product and will make your final results equally consistent.

Butter:

Be sure to use unsalted butter for all the recipes in this book. Do not substitute margarine, as it will not produce the correct results.

Chocolate and Cocoa Powder:

I used Guittard chocolate chips, bars, and cocoa powder for all of the recipes in this book. They are a good-quality chocolate, sold for a good price and made by a family-run operation in San Francisco. If you are making cocoa pâte à choux or chocolate glaze, I suggest you use Dutch-processed cocoa powder (a.k.a. alkalized cocoa powder), which has a stronger flavor and a darker color. If you don't

have it on hand or can't find it, natural cocoa powder will still work just fine. You may notice your cocoa pâte à choux or glaze is a little bit lighter in color, but it will still taste delicious.

Edible Glitters, Sprinkles, Dragées, Sanding Sugars, Luster Dusts, and Petal Dusts:

There are no rules when it comes to decorations, so get creative with your pastries! Chef Rubber has an incredible array of options, as does N.Y. Cake (see Retail Therapy, page 284).

Fine Sea Salt:

La Baleine fine sea salt is my standard salt for baking, but you can use regular table salt for all of the recipes if you wish.

Fresh Fruits:

It is always best to bake with fruits when they're in season, so that the fruit in your recipes tastes the absolute best. Shop at your local farmers' market for the cream of the crop.

Frozen Puff Pastry:

If you can find frozen puff pastry that is made from all butter (versus butter and shortening), you will like your Gâteaux Saint-Honoré even better. I like Dufour brand, which is available in most Whole Foods grocery stores.

Gel Paste Food Colorings:

I used AmeriColor Soft Gel Paste for all the glaze recipes in this book.

Gold and Silver Leaf:

These decorations are quite pricey, so remember that a little goes a long way. You can also substitute them with less expensive decorations, like gold edible glitter or sprinkles.

Heavy Cream:

For whipped cream, try to find a heavy cream that does not include additives such as guar gum. Some brands of organic heavy cream are available without gums. I find these additives give whipped cream a slightly grainy texture. As for the rest of the recipes, use whichever heavy cream you like best.

Instant Espresso Powder:

I prefer Medaglia d'Oro Instant Espresso Coffee for my coffee-flavored recipes, but any brand of instant espresso or coffee will work just as well.

Milk:

For pâte à choux dough, you can substitute low-fat milk, but not nonfat. For the pastry cream or ice cream recipes, it is best to use whole milk for a rich and creamy texture.

Nut Butters and Nut Pastes:

For the best flavor use the highest-quality nut butters or nut pastes you can find. Gourmet or specialty food retailers are your best source.

Vanilla Beans:

I'm in love with vanilla beans from Singing Dog Vanilla in Eugene, Oregon. Their beans are organic, sustainably sourced, and sold at a great price. Store your vanilla beans in a resealable bag in the freezer to keep them fresh for up to a year.

Xanthan Gum:

Because of the popularity of gluten-free baking, xanthan gum isn't too hard to find. Check your local natural foods store to see if they have it in stock. Bob's Red Mill is probably the most widely distributed brand. And don't worry about buying xanthan gum even if you don't plan to use it a lot; it has a 24-month shelf life.

I use xanthan gum in my recipes for ice cream, a more modern (and super-easy!) method. I find it makes for a softer, creamier textured ice cream, especially when using a home ice cream maker. If you prefer, you can substitute the xanthan gum and cornstarch with 4 large egg yolks and cook the ice cream base following the classic tempering cooking method.

Tools

DE LA TRADE

Baking Sheets:

I recommend using commercial-quality 18-by-13-inch aluminum baking sheets (a.k.a. bun pans or half-sheet pans). They are durable, inexpensive, and a heavy gauge, which will make for evenly baked goods.

Heat-Resistant Rubber Spatula:

Invest in a good-quality silicone or high-heat-resistant (up to 400°F) rubber spatula. It is the tool most often used in the recipes in this cookbook, and essential to cooking pâte à choux dough without melting a spatula in the process. It is also the best tool for folding mousses, filling pastry bags, and scraping bowls absolutely clean. Le Creuset silicone spatulas are my favorite, and I never bake or cook without one handy.

Parchment Paper:

Whatever you do, do not substitute waxed paper for parchment paper. The waxed paper will leave a film on your baked pâte à choux.

Pastry Bags:

I prefer plastic pastry bags, even though they are not the most eco-friendly. This is because they are the most commonly used type of pastry bag in professional kitchens and what I am used to. If you prefer cloth pastry bags, all of the recipes will work perfectly fine with them.

Piping Tips:

I use Ateco piping tips for all the recipes in this book. You can use any brand you prefer, so long as they are the same shape and size.

Plastic Bowl Scraper:

This is a great $1 purchase. I use it to transfer pâte à choux dough to a pastry bag.

Pots and Pans:

I exclusively use All-Clad stainless steel pots and pans for my cooking, but any brand of good-quality, heavy stainless steel is fine for cooking the pâte à choux dough and pastry cream recipes in this cookbook. When using a nonstick pan, note the difference in cooking time in the recipe.

The Pastry Tips

- It's best to sift the bread flour before using it. This will prevent lumps from forming in the dough.

- Use a heavyweight saucepan for cooking your pâte à choux. It will ensure more even heat distribution as you cook the dough.

- I use whole milk for my pâte à choux, but if you only have low-fat milk on hand, that's fine to use instead.

- Make sure you bring the water, milk, butter, salt, and sugar mixture to a full rolling boil. This will help with some of the evaporation, and the quick cooking, needed to make great pâte à choux.

- Just dump all the flour into the pot at once. Seriously, it is not going to cause an issue.

- After adding the flour, be sure to stir your dough in the pot constantly, but not vigorously (unless you want arms like a drummer!). Continue to cook the dough until you see a light golden-colored skin on the bottom of the saucepan.

- Adding the eggs is when it's time to stir vigorously (drummer arms!). Don't worry: You can't overmix pâte à choux.

- To save a few minutes, you can transfer the cooked dough to the bowl of a stand mixer fitted with the paddle attachment, and add the eggs one at a time. Be sure to mix the dough on the lowest speed and scrape down the sides of the bowl between the addition of each egg.

- When letting your dough cool before using it, you don't need to cover the bowl. Just let it stand at room temperature.

- If you would prefer to make pâte à choux dough in advance, you can store the cooled dough in an airtight container in the refrigerator for up to 1 day before piping and baking.

PIPING YOUR PÂTE À CHOUX—YOU'RE HALFWAY THERE

- Pâte à choux dough is sticky stuff. When filling your pastry bag, fold the bag down in order to place the dough in the bottom of the bag.

- Use a plastic bowl scraper to push the dough toward the piping tip in the pastry bag. This will also help push air bubbles out of the pastry bag, which can affect your piping. Twist the back of the bag closed to prevent the dough from escaping when piping. Alternatively, you can use a strip of plastic wrap to tie the bag tightly closed.

- Dab a fingertip's worth of pâte à choux dough on each corner of the baking sheet to help secure the parchment paper. This will prevent the parchment paper from lifting off the baking sheet as you are piping.

- When piping éclairs, use a ruler and pencil on the parchment to create straight lines as a piping guide. But be sure to turn the paper over so the pencil marks are on the underside before piping. For cream puffs or Paris-Brest shapes, a set of round cookie cutters, small ramekins, cups, or any other circular household item can be used as a guide. Remember: Piping takes practice!

- To properly hold a pastry bag, use your dominant hand to hold the bag. Squeeze your hand like you are making a fist on the back of the bag to squeeze the dough out of the bag evenly. Use your non-dominant hand to steady the bag as you pipe your shape. If your wrist hurts from piping, try filling the pastry bag less full. Piping thick dough can strain your wrist if you don't pipe very often.

- Always stop the pressure on the piping bag before lifting the pastry tip away from your piped shape—this will prevent peaks and points from forming. If you do have unwanted peaks and points, dip your fingertip in a bit of cold water and smooth the dough.

- If you're not happy with your piped shapes, not to worry! Just scrape up the dough from the parchment paper, put the dough back into the pastry bag, and pipe it again.

BAKING PÂTE À CHOUX—THE FINAL STEP

- Remember: The larger the shape of pâte à choux, the more it will puff. Be sure to leave about 1 inch of space between small cream puffs and small éclair shells and about 2 inches of space between large cream puffs, large éclairs, and Paris-Brest shells.

- Be sure to bake the pâte à choux in an oven with the convection setting off. The fan of a convection oven can cause pâte à choux to rise too quickly and unevenly. Additionally, the convection fan can cause the exteriors of the pâte à choux to bake too quickly.

- I always set a timer for the halfway point in a recipe's bake time. This reminds me to rotate the baking sheet, if needed, and assess just how much more time my dessert needs to bake. Because all ovens can operate a little differently, you may find that your pâte à choux needs to bake for a bit more time, or a bit less, to achieve the desired results.

- When baking cocoa pâte à choux, it can be difficult to determine when it is done. As the dough begins to dry out, it will have a matte surface where tiny cracks will appear.

- To determine if your pâte à choux is fully baked, remove a shell from the oven and place on a cooling rack at room temperature. If it deflates, it is too moist on the inside and needs more time to bake. If it holds its shape, tear it open. If the center is still very moist and gummy, continue to let it bake until the center dries out almost completely.

- Baking pâte à choux in advance is one of the best things about this dough—it stores really well! You can store the baked pâte à choux in an airtight container for up to 3 days at room temperature, or in the freezer for up to 3 weeks.

- Is it best to "refresh" baked and unfilled pâte à choux shells in the oven or toaster oven if you make them in advance. This will help them crisp back up. I suggest preheating an oven to 350°F and baking room temperature shells for 5 to 8 minutes, or frozen shells for about 12 minutes.

PASTRY CREAMS—THE CRÈME DE LA CRÈME

- Save the egg whites left over from pastry cream recipes to make meringue! (Or, save the yolks left over from meringue recipes to make pastry cream!)

- Remember to use a heavyweight saucepan when making pastry cream. It will ensure more even heat distribution and offer less opportunity for overcooking.

- Set the bowl of eggs and cornstarch on a folded kitchen towel when adding the hot milk to hold the bowl in place while whisking.

- It is very important to be able to judge the thickness of pastry cream while you are cooking it. Whisk the mixture slowly until just thickened—this will prevent a layer of foamy bubbles from forming in the pot, something that can make it difficult to determine the thickness of the pastry cream. Once the pastry cream is thickened and shows signs of lumps, then you can increase the speed of whisking to help smooth out the texture of the pastry cream.

- Do not mistake lumps in your pastry cream for scrambled eggs—sometimes you just need to whisk the cream more vigorously to smooth it out.

- Don't forget to add the butter to your pastry cream! It's really easy to forget, especially if you are concerned about immediately straining the cream. If you happen to forget, you can add the butter to the pastry cream after it has been strained.

LES GLAZES

- If you don't like using corn syrup, you can use a light-colored honey instead. But keep in mind that your glaze will have a light honey flavor.

- When mixing the glaze, do not whisk too vigorously. That would create lots of bubbles in your glaze. However, if you end up with bubbles on your glazed pastries, use a toothpick to pop them while the glaze is still wet.

- When coloring glazes, add the color one drop at a time—you can always add more, but you can never take it away. If you need just a tiny bit more color, dip the tip of a toothpick into the coloring and stir into the glaze.

- If you don't want drips of glaze on your cream puffs or éclairs, hold the dipped pastries upside down until all the excess glaze drips away before inverting. Use a clean fingertip to wipe away any glaze that drips down the sides.

- To set the glaze more quickly, you can place your glazed pastries in the refrigerator for about 10 minutes. Otherwise, let them set up at room temperature for about 20 minutes.

- Your glaze should have a thick consistency that still allows for dipping. To make a thicker glaze, add sifted confectioners' sugar until the glaze reaches the desired consistency. To make a thinner glaze, add water, 1 teaspoon at a time.

ASSEMBLING YOUR PASTRY MASTERPIECES

- The best way to approach the recipes in this cookbook is to make the fillings first. While they are chilling or setting, make the pâte à choux. And make the glaze just before you are ready to use it.

- I use the same piping tip to pierce the holes in my cream puff and éclair shells as I do to fill them. However, if you have a bismarck tip (or a doughnut filling pastry tip), you can pierce and fill your shells in one step!

- If you find that using a pastry tip to pierce holes in your cream puff or éclair shells is causing them to crack, switch to using the tip of a paring knife to create a little hole for the filling.

- To fill cream puff or éclair shells completely full, pipe the filling into the shell until it feels heavy and you can see the cream just squeezing out at the opening of the hole.

- If you want to get ahead, you can make most of the components for any individual recipe and store them separately until you are ready to assemble your pastries. This will create pastries with the best texture.

SERVING AND STORAGE—IT'S TIME TO EAT!

- Assembled pâte à choux pastries are best when served within a few hours of assembly. However, most can be stored for up to 8 hours before getting soft. Keep in mind, the assembled pastries won't go bad if stored overnight, but they will lose most of their crisp texture.

- I prefer to store my assembled pastries on a platter or in a paper cake box when storing them in the refrigerator. Attempting to cover them with plastic wrap usually just messes up all the decorations.

The Basics

Pâte à Choux Dough

MAKES ENOUGH FOR
16 TO 18 SMALL ÉCLAIR SHELLS
10 TO 12 LARGE ÉCLAIR SHELLS
30 TO 36 SMALL CREAM PUFF SHELLS
14 TO 16 LARGE CREAM PUFF SHELLS
OR 8 TO 10 PARIS-BREST SHELLS

⅓ cup (80 grams) water

⅓ cup (80 grams) whole milk

5 tablespoons (70 grams) unsalted butter, cut into small pieces

1 teaspoon sugar

¼ teaspoon salt

¾ cup (105 grams) bread flour, sifted

3 large eggs

1   In a medium saucepan, bring the water, milk, butter, sugar, and salt to a rolling boil and cook until the butter has melted. Turn off the heat and add the flour all at once. Using a heat-resistant rubber spatula, stir the mixture until no lumps of dry flour remain, 1 to 2 minutes.

2   Turn the heat to medium and cook the dough, stirring constantly, until it forms a ball and leaves a skin on the base of the pot, 3 to 4 minutes. (If using a nonstick pan, a skin may not form on the base of the pot. Simply set a timer for 4 minutes instead.)

3   Transfer the dough to a large bowl and stir to cool the dough just slightly, about 2 minutes. Add the eggs, one at a time, stirring vigorously until the mixture is smooth. Scrape down the sides of the bowl with the rubber spatula

between each addition of egg. Once the dough is fully combined, let it stand at room temperature to cool for about 10 minutes.

4   Pipe and bake shells as directed on pages 31 to 36.

Cocoa Pâte à Choux Dough

Add 2 tablespoons (15 grams) cocoa powder, sifted, with the bread flour when making the dough. Proceed as directed, cooking the dough in Step 2 for a full 4 minutes.

MAKING PÂTE À CHOUX

ADD THE WATER, MILK, BUTTER, SUGAR, AND SALT TO THE SAUCEPAN

BRING THE INGREDIENTS TO A ROLLING BOIL

COOK UNTIL THE BUTTER HAS MELTED

TURN OFF THE HEAT AND ADD THE FLOUR ALL AT ONCE

STIR IN THE FLOUR

COOK UNTIL THE DOUGH FORMS A BALL AND LEAVES A SKIN ON THE BOTTOM OF THE POT

TRANSFER THE DOUGH TO A BOWL AND ADD THE EGGS, ONE AT A TIME

STIR VIGOROUSLY UNTIL THE DOUGH IS SMOOTH

LET COOL FOR ABOUT 10 MINUTES

For Small Éclair Shells

1   Preheat the oven to 350°F. Line a baking sheet with parchment paper.

2   Fill a pastry bag fitted with a star piping tip (such as Ateco #866) with the pâte à choux dough or cocoa pâte à choux dough and pipe straight lines, 3 inches long and ¾ inch wide, onto the baking sheet, leaving about 1 inch of space between each. (If desired, use a ruler to draw 3-inch-wide columns on the parchment paper to serve as a tracing guide when piping. Be sure to place the parchment paper marked side down on the baking sheet before piping the éclairs.) Lightly moisten a fingertip with cold water and gently smooth any peaks or points created when piping.

3   Bake for 35 to 40 minutes, until deep golden brown and cooked through in the center. Let cool on the baking sheet to room temperature.

PIPING AND BAKING PÂTE À CHOUX SHAPES

FOLD THE TOP EDGE OF THE PASTRY BAG DOWN AND FILL WITH DOUGH

USE A PLASTIC BOWL SCRAPER TO PUSH THE DOUGH TOWARD THE PIPING TIP

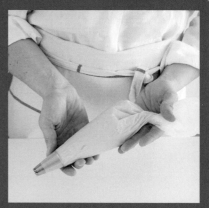

TWIST THE TOP OF THE BAG CLOSED

TRACE DESIRED SHAPES ONTO THE PARCHMENT AND FLIP THE PAPER OVER

DAB PÂTE À CHOUX DOUGH ONTO THE CORNERS TO SECURE THE PARCHMENT

HOLD THE PASTRY BAG STRAIGHT UP AND DOWN TO PIPE MOUNDS FOR CREAM PUFFS

PIPE DOUGH INTO RINGS FOR PARIS-BREST SHELLS

HOLD THE PASTRY BAG AT AN ANGLE TO PIPE ÉCLAIR SHELLS

USE A MOISTENED FINGERTIP TO SMOOTH ANY PEAKS OR POINTS

For Large Éclair Shells

1   Preheat the oven to 350°F. Line a baking sheet with parchment paper.

2   Fill a pastry bag fitted with a star piping tip (such as Ateco #868) with the pâte à choux dough or cocoa pâte à choux dough and pipe straight lines, 5 inches long and 1 inch wide, onto the baking sheet, leaving about 2 inches of space between each. (If desired, use a ruler to draw 5-inch-wide columns on the parchment paper to serve as a tracing guide when piping. Be sure to place the parchment paper marked side down on the baking sheet before piping the éclairs.) Lightly moisten a fingertip with cold water and gently smooth any peaks or points created when piping.

3   Bake for 50 to 55 minutes, until deep golden brown and cooked through in the center. Let cool on the baking sheet to room temperature.

For Small Cream Puff Shells

1 Preheat the oven to 350°F. Line two baking sheets with parchment paper.

2 Fill a pastry bag fitted with a round piping tip (such as Ateco #806) with the pâte à choux dough or cocoa pâte à choux dough and pipe small mounds, 1¼ inches in diameter and 1 inch tall, leaving about 1 inch of space between each mound. (If desired, use a 1¼-inch round cookie cutter to trace circles on the parchment paper to serve as a guide when piping. Be sure to place the parchment paper marked side down on the baking sheets before piping the cream puffs.) Lightly moisten a fingertip with cold water and gently smooth any peaks or points created when piping.

3 Bake for 35 to 40 minutes, until deep golden brown and cooked through in the center. Let cool on the baking sheets to room temperature.

For Large Cream Puff Shells

1   Preheat the oven to 350°F. Line a baking sheet with parchment paper.

2   Fill a pastry bag fitted with a round piping tip (such as Ateco #809) with the pâte à choux dough or cocoa pâte à choux dough and pipe mounds, 1¾ inches in diameter and 1¼ inches tall, leaving about 1 inch of space between each mound. (If desired, use a 1¾-inch round cookie cutter to trace circles on the parchment paper to serve as a guide when piping. Be sure to place the parchment paper marked side down on the baking sheet before piping the cream puffs.) Lightly moisten a fingertip with cold water and gently smooth any peaks or points created when piping.

3   Bake for 45 to 50 minutes, until deep golden brown and cooked through in the center. Let cool on the baking sheet to room temperature.

For Paris-Brest Shells

1 Preheat the oven to 350°F. Line a baking sheet with parchment paper.

2 Fill a pastry bag fitted with a star piping tip (such as Ateco #827) with the pâte à choux dough or cocoa pâte à choux dough and pipe rings 2¾ inches in diameter, leaving about 1 inch of space between each ring. (If desired, use a 2¾-inch round cookie cutter to trace circles on the parchment paper to serve as a guide when piping. Be sure to place the parchment paper marked side down on the baking sheet before piping the shells.) Lightly moisten a fingertip with cold water and gently smooth any peaks or points created when piping.

3 Bake for 45 to 50 minutes, until deep golden brown and cooked through in the center. Let cool on the baking sheet to room temperature.

Vanilla Bean Pastry Cream

1 In a large bowl, whisk the egg yolks, egg, and cornstarch until completely smooth.

2 In a medium pot, bring the milk, sugar, salt, and vanilla seeds to a boil. Slowly pour the hot milk over the egg yolk mixture while whisking constantly. Return the mixture to the pot and cook over medium-low heat, whisking constantly but slowly, until just thickened and bubbles rise to the surface, about 4 minutes. Increase the speed of whisking to smooth the custard and cook until it has thickened to the consistency of pudding and coats the back of a spoon, about 2 more minutes.

3 Remove the pot from the heat, add the butter, and whisk until fully melted and smooth. Strain through a fine-mesh sieve into a large bowl and cover the pastry cream with plastic wrap directly on the surface to prevent a skin from forming. Refrigerate until cold and fully set, about 2 hours, or up to 3 days.

4 large egg yolks

1 large egg

¼ cup plus 3 tablespoons (53 grams) cornstarch

2 cups (480 grams) whole milk

½ cup plus 2 tablespoons (126 grams) sugar

¼ teaspoon salt

Seeds from 1 vanilla bean

5 tablespoons (70 grams) unsalted butter, cut into small pieces

Note *You can substitute 2 teaspoons of vanilla extract for the vanilla bean. Add the extract with the butter in Step 3.*

Chocolate Pastry Cream

1   In a large bowl, whisk the egg yolks, egg, and cornstarch until completely smooth.

2   In a medium pot, bring the milk, sugar, and salt to a boil. Slowly pour the hot milk over the egg yolks while whisking constantly. Return the mixture to the pot and cook over medium-low heat, whisking constantly but slowly, until just thickened and bubbles rise to the surface, about 4 minutes. Increase the speed of whisking to smooth the custard and cook until it has thickened to the consistency of pudding and coats the back of a spoon, about 2 more minutes.

3   Remove the pot from the heat, add the chocolate and butter, and whisk until fully melted and smooth. Strain through a fine-mesh sieve into a bowl and cover the pastry cream with plastic wrap directly on the surface to prevent a skin from forming. Refrigerate until cold and fully set, about 2 hours, or up to 3 days.

4 large egg yolks

1 large egg

¼ cup (30 grams) cornstarch

2 cups (480 grams) whole milk

½ cup (100 grams) sugar

¼ teaspoon salt

1 cup (170 grams) bittersweet chocolate, chopped or chips

5 tablespoons (70 grams) unsalted butter, cut into small pieces

Chocolate Glaze

Sift the confectioners' sugar and cocoa powder into a large bowl. Add the remaining ingredients and whisk by hand until smooth. To make a thicker glaze, slowly add sifted confectioners' sugar until you reach the desired consistency. To make a thinner glaze, add water, 1 teaspoon at a time, to reach the desired consistency. Cover the bowl with plastic wrap and set aside at room temperature until ready to use, or up to 1 day.

1½ cups (180 grams) confectioners' sugar, plus more for adjusting glaze

¼ cup (30 grams) cocoa powder

¼ cup (60 grams) water, plus more for adjusting glaze

2 tablespoons (40 grams) light corn syrup

¼ teaspoon salt

Note The glaze should create a nearly opaque coating on the tops of the shells that are being glazed—thick enough so the shell is barely visible through the glaze, yet thin enough to allow for dipping with ease. You may find you need to adjust the consistency as you are working with the glaze, as well.

White Glaze

Sift the confectioners' sugar into a large bowl. Add the water, corn syrup, and salt and whisk by hand until smooth. To thicken the glaze, slowly add sifted confectioners' sugar until the glaze reaches the desired consistency. To thin, add water, 1 teaspoon at a time. To tint the glaze, if desired, add food coloring, one drop at a time, stirring until evenly combined, until the glaze reaches the desired color. Cover the bowl with plastic wrap and set aside at room temperature until ready to use, up to 1 day.

1½ cups (180 grams) confectioners' sugar, plus more for adjusting glaze

¼ cup (60 grams) water, plus more for adjusting glaze

2 tablespoons (40 grams) light corn syrup

¼ teaspoon salt

Gel-paste food coloring (optional)

Note *The glaze should create a nearly opaque coating on the tops of the shells that are being glazed—thick enough so the shell is barely visible through the glaze, yet thin enough to allow for dipping with ease. You may find you need to adjust the consistency as you are working with the glaze, as well.*

Whipped Cream

MAKES ABOUT 4 CUPS

By hand or using a stand mixer fitted with the whisk attachment, whip the cream and confectioners' sugar until stiff peaks form. Cover and refrigerate until ready to use, up to 2 hours. If the whipped cream softens while sitting in the refrigerator, re-whip until stiff peaks form before using.

2 cups (480 grams) heavy whipping cream

½ cup (60 grams) confectioners' sugar, sifted

Royal Icing

MAKES 2½ CUPS

In a large bowl, whisk all the ingredients until smooth. Cover the bowl tightly with plastic wrap until ready to use, up to 2 hours.

4 cups (480 grams) confectioners' sugar, sifted

½ teaspoon cream of tartar

3 large egg whites

Classic

Cream Puffs

▷ MAKES 14 TO 16 LARGE CREAM PUFFS ◁

1 Fill a pastry bag fitted with a star piping tip (such as Ateco #826) with the whipped cream and refrigerate until ready to use.

2 Using a serrated knife, cut the cream puff shells in half horizontally. Pipe a generous mound of the whipped cream on the base of each cream puff. Gently place the top of the cream puff on the cream. Serve immediately, or refrigerate for up to 4 hours. Lightly dust with confectioners' sugar just before serving.

Note These classic cream puffs are filled with lightly sweetened whipped cream, but you can always doctor them up a bit. Sifted cocoa powder, almond extract, or a little lemon zest in the whipped cream make for fun filling additions!

Whipped Cream (page 41)

14 to 16 Large Cream Puff Shells (page 35)

Confectioners' sugar, for dusting

Classic Éclairs

1 Place a round piping tip (such as Ateco #802) on the tip of your index finger, or use the tip of a paring knife, and pierce three ¼-inch holes in the bottom of each éclair shell.

2 Fill a pastry bag fitted with the same round piping tip with the pastry cream. Piping into the holes in each éclair, gently fill with pastry cream.

3 Dip the top one-third of each éclair into the glaze, allowing the excess glaze to drip away from the éclair before inverting. Decorate with gold leaf and chopped chocolate, if desired. Set aside at room temperature until the glaze has fully set and hardened, about 20 minutes. As you are dipping the éclairs, adjust the thickness of the glaze as needed (see page 25). Serve immediately, or refrigerate for up to 8 hours.

10 to 12 Large Éclair Shells (page 33)

Vanilla Bean Pastry Cream (page 37)

Chocolate Glaze (page 39)

Edible gold leaf, for decorating (optional)

Bittersweet chocolate, finely chopped, for decorating (optional)

Note *Edible gold leaf can be found at specialty baking and pastry retailers (see Retail Therapy, page 284).*

▲ *Classic Éclairs and Double Espresso Éclairs (page 73)*

Chouquettes

1 Preheat the oven to 350°F. Line two baking sheets with parchment paper.

2 Fill a pastry bag fitted with a round piping tip (such as Ateco #806) with the pâte à choux dough and pipe small mounds, about 1¼ inches in diameter and 1 inch tall, onto the baking sheets, leaving about 1 inch of space between each mound. Lightly brush the tops of each mound with the beaten egg and sprinkle generously with the pearl sugar. Bake for 35 to 40 minutes, until puffed and golden brown. Serve warm.

Pâte à Choux Dough (page 28)

1 large egg, lightly beaten

¼ cup (56 grams) pearl sugar

Note Chouquettes can be made 3 days ahead and refrigerated in an airtight container, or frozen for up to 1 month. If made in advance, preheat the oven to 300°F and reheat until just warm and crisp, about 10 minutes, before serving.

Chantilly Swans

1 Preheat the oven to 350°F. Line two baking sheets with parchment paper.

2 **For the swan bodies:** Fit a pastry bag with a large round piping tip (such as Ateco #809) and fill with three-quarters of the pâte à choux dough. Pipe 14 large teardrops of dough, about 2 inches long and ¾ inch tall, on one of the baking sheets, leaving about 1 inch of space between each teardrop.

3 **For the swan necks and heads:** Fit a second pastry bag with a smaller round piping tip (such as Ateco #803) and fill with the remaining one-quarter of the pâte à choux dough. On the second baking sheet, pipe 14 or more small shapes similar to the numeral "2" and about 2 inches long. Start at the top end with a small dot of dough (the head) and then continue without stopping, slightly curving to form the rest of the "2" (the neck). Then, dip your fingertips into cold water and pinch the base of the dot to create a round head that is

Pâte à Choux Dough (page 28)

Chantilly Cream (page 53)

Note *When you are piping the swan necks and heads, don't become frustrated. They often look strange on the baking sheet. But once you assemble your little birdies, they will become super cute!*

defined from the rest of the neck. Dip your fingertips into cold water again, and pinch the very tip of the head to create a pointed beak.

4 Transfer both baking sheets to the oven; bake until deep golden brown, 20 to 25 minutes for the swan necks and heads and about 15 minutes longer for the swan bodies. Let cool to room temperature.

5 Fill a pastry bag fitted with a star piping tip (such as Ateco #826) with the chantilly cream and refrigerate until ready to use.

6 Using a serrated knife, cut the swan bodies in half horizontally. Cut each top half into 2 pieces, lengthwise, for the wings. Pipe 2 mounds of chantilly cream on the bottom of each swan body, making the one in back slightly higher. Place two wing pieces on the back of the cream. Place a swan neck and head into the smaller mound of cream on each body, anchoring the base of the neck at the point where the wings meet. Serve immediately, or refrigerate for up to 8 hours.

CHANTILLY CREAM

By hand or using a stand mixer fitted with the whisk attachment, whip the cream, confectioners' sugar, and vanilla until stiff peaks form. Cover and refrigerate until ready to use, up to 2 hours. If the cream softens while sitting in the refrigerator, re-whip until stiff peaks form before using.

1½ cups (360 grams) heavy whipping cream

3 tablespoons (21 grams) confectioners' sugar, sifted

1 teaspoon vanilla extract

Religieuses

1   Preheat the oven to 350°F. Line two baking sheets with parchment paper.

2   **For the small cream puffs:** Fit a pastry bag with a round piping tip (such as Ateco #806) and fill with two-thirds of the pâte à choux dough. Pipe 18 small mounds, about 1¼ inches in diameter and 1 inch tall, on one of the baking sheets, leaving about 1 inch of space between each mound. Bake for 40 to 45 minutes, until deep golden brown and cooked through in the center. Let cool on the baking sheet to room temperature.

3   **For the miniature cream puffs:** Fit a second pastry bag with a round piping tip (such as Ateco #804) and fill with the remaining one-third of the pâte à choux dough. Pipe 18 tiny mounds, about ¾ inch in diameter and ½ inch tall, on the other baking sheet, leaving about ½ inch of space between each mound. Bake for 35 to 40 minutes, until deep golden brown and cooked through in the center. Let cool on the baking sheet to room temperature.

Pâte à Choux Dough (page 28)

Chocolate Pastry Cream (page 38)

Chocolate Glaze (page 39)

Note Oftentimes, religieuses also include chocolate buttercream piped between the cream puffs. But I omitted the buttercream here because you need so little of it, and I find an extra recipe just makes these pastries too fussy. Less is more.

4   Place a round piping tip (such as Ateco #802) on the tip of your index finger, or use the tip of a paring knife, and pierce a ¼-inch hole in the bottom of each of the small and miniature cream puffs.

5   Fill a pastry bag fitted with the same round piping tip with the pastry cream. Piping into the hole in each of the small and miniature cream puffs, gently fill with pastry cream. Reserve the remaining pastry cream in the refrigerator until ready to assemble the religieuses.

6   Dip the top one-third of each cream puff into the glaze, allowing excess glaze to drip away from the cream puff before inverting. Set aside until the glaze has fully set and hardened, about 20 minutes. As you are dipping the cream puffs, adjust the thickness of the glaze as needed (see page 25).

7   **To assemble the religieuses:** Pipe a ¼-inch round dollop of the pastry cream on the top of each small cream puff. Set a miniature cream puff on the pastry cream, pressing gently to stabilize. Decoratively pipe a small dot of the pastry cream on the top of each religieuse. Serve immediately, or refrigerate for up to 8 hours.

Classic Profiteroles

MAKES 9 SERVINGS

1 Remove the ice cream from freezer to soften. Slice the cream puff shells in half horizontally, setting the top of each cream puff next to its corresponding bottom.

2 Using an ice cream scoop dipped into warm water, place a scoop of ice cream on the bottom of each cream puff, then set the top of each cream puff on the ice cream. Place the assembled profiteroles on a baking sheet and transfer to the freezer to set, about 20 minutes.

3 **To serve:** Set three profiteroles on a serving dish and drizzle with the chocolate sauce. Place one more profiterole on top to create a small pyramid. Drizzle with more chocolate sauce and serve immediately.

Vanilla Bean Ice Cream (page 59), or 2 pints store-bought

36 Small Cream Puff Shells (page 34)

Chocolate Sauce (page 59)

Note Remember: You're not lazy if you buy vanilla ice cream or even the chocolate sauce! Instead, consider yourself time efficient.

VANILLA BEAN ICE CREAM

1 In a medium pot, whisk the sugar, cornstarch, xanthan gum, and salt until well combined. Add the milk, cream, and vanilla seeds and bring to a simmer. Cook, whisking occasionally, until thickened, 8 to 10 minutes. Strain the mixture through a fine-mesh sieve into a large metal bowl. Place the bowl of ice cream base over another bowl filled with ice water and stir the base until cooled to room temperature. Refrigerate until cold, about 2 hours.

2 Freeze the ice cream base in an ice cream machine according to the manufacturer's instructions until the ice cream has a smooth, soft-serve texture. Store in the freezer for 4 hours to set before serving.

½ cup (100 grams) sugar

1 tablespoon (8 grams) cornstarch

½ teaspoon xanthan gum

¼ teaspoon salt

2 cups (480 grams) whole milk

1½ cups (360 grams) heavy whipping cream

Seeds from 1 vanilla bean

Note To make coffee ice cream, replace the vanilla with 3 tablespoons (18 grams) finely ground coffee.

CHOCOLATE SAUCE

1 Place the chocolate in a medium bowl.

2 In a small saucepan, bring the cream, corn syrup, and salt to a boil. Remove from the heat, pour over the chocolate, and add the vanilla. Let the mixture stand for 2 minutes to soften the chocolate, then whisk until smooth. Serve warm.

1⅓ cups (227 grams) semisweet chocolate, chopped or chips

1 cup (240 grams) heavy whipping cream

2 tablespoons (40 grams) light corn syrup

¼ teaspoon salt

1 teaspoon vanilla extract

Praline Paris-Brests

1 Preheat the oven to 350°F. Line a baking sheet with parchment paper.

2 Fill a pastry bag fitted with a star piping tip (such as Ateco #827) with pâte à choux and pipe rings 2¾ inches in diameter on the baking sheet, leaving about 1 inch of space between each ring. (If desired, use a cookie cutter to trace circles on the parchment before piping. Be sure to place the parchment paper marked side down on the baking sheet.) Lightly brush the rings with the beaten egg and sprinkle with the almonds. Bake for 40 to 45 minutes, until deep golden brown and cooked through in the center. Let cool on the baking sheet to room temperature.

3 Using a serrated knife, slice the Paris-Brests in half horizontally. Fill a pastry bag fitted with a star piping tip with the pastry cream and pipe rings onto the Paris-Brest bases. Place the top of each Paris-Brest on the pastry cream. Lightly dust with confectioners' sugar. Serve immediately, or refrigerate for up to 1 day.

Pâte à Choux Dough (page 28)

1 large egg, lightly beaten

¾ cup (90 grams) sliced almonds

Praline Pastry Cream (page 62)

Confectioners' sugar, for dusting

Note Get creative! If you love pistachios best, you can always fill your Paris-Brests with pistachio pastry cream (page 116) and top them with chopped pistachios, or swap the filling for chocolate pastry cream (page 38) and glaze with chocolate glaze (page 39). Paris-Brest shells can be used for any flavor combination you like.

PRALINE PASTRY CREAM

1 In a large bowl, whisk the egg yolks, egg, and cornstarch until completely smooth.

2 In a medium pot, bring the milk, sugar, and salt to a boil. Slowly pour the hot milk over the egg yolks while whisking constantly. Return the mixture to the pot and cook over medium-low heat, whisking constantly but slowly, until just thickened and bubbles rise to the surface, about 4 minutes. Increase the speed of whisking to smooth the custard and continue to cook until it has thickened to the consistency of pudding and coats the back of a spoon, about 2 more minutes.

3 Immediately remove the pot from the heat, add the praline paste and butter, and whisk until fully melted and smooth. Strain the mixture through a fine-mesh sieve into a large bowl and cover the pastry cream with a sheet of plastic wrap directly on the surface to prevent a skin from forming. Refrigerate until cold and fully set, about 2 hours, or up to 3 days.

4 large egg yolks

1 large egg

¼ cup plus 2 tablespoons (45 grams) cornstarch

2 cups (480 grams) whole milk

½ cup plus 2 tablespoons (126 grams) sugar

¼ teaspoon salt

½ cup (150 grams) praline paste

5 tablespoons (70 grams) unsalted butter, cut into small pieces

Note Praline paste, made of equal parts roasted almonds and hazelnuts, is a popular ingredient in French desserts. However, if praline paste isn't readily available to you, either hazelnut paste or almond butter will substitute very nicely.

Pets de Nonne

1 In a medium saucepan, bring the water, milk, butter, sugar, and salt to a rolling boil. Turn off the heat and add the flour all at once, while continuing to stir. Turn the heat to medium-low and cook the dough, while stirring constantly, until it forms a ball and leaves a skin on the base of the pot, 3 to 4 minutes.

2 Transfer the dough to a large bowl. Add the whole eggs, one at a time, stirring vigorously to combine between each addition. Scrape down the sides of the bowl with a rubber spatula as needed between each addition. Add the egg whites and mix the dough until the eggs are fully combined and the mixture is smooth.

3 **To fry the pets de nonne:** Heat 2 inches of oil in a heavy pot to 375°F on an instant-read thermometer. Sift the confectioners' sugar into a large bowl. Place a rack on a baking sheet.

½ **cup (120 grams) water**

½ **cup (120 grams) whole milk**

6 tablespoons (85 grams) unsalted butter

1 tablespoon (13 grams) granulated sugar

¼ **teaspoon salt**

1 cup (128 grams) unbleached all-purpose flour

3 large eggs

2 large egg whites

Canola oil, for frying

1 to 2 cups (120 to 240 grams) confectioners' sugar, for coating

4 Using a ¾- to 1-ounce-size cookie scoop, carefully drop one scoop of dough at a time into the oil. Continue to add more dough to the oil, taking care to leave about 1 inch of space between each piece. Fry the dough until deep golden brown, 4 to 7 minutes. Using a slotted spoon, carefully remove the pets de nonne from the oil, allowing the excess oil to drain back into the pot. Immediately transfer them to the bowl of confectioners' sugar and gently toss to completely coat. Set on the rack to cool, or serve immediately.

Note *This recipe cracks me up each time I make it.* Pets de nonne *translates to nuns' farts?! Of course their little puffs would be confectioners' sugar-coated and just heavenly.*

◀ *Pets de Nonne and French Crullers (page 70)*

Gâteaux Saint-Honoré

1 Preheat the oven to 375°F. Line a baking sheet with parchment paper.

2 On a lightly floured surface, roll out the puff pastry to ⅛ inch thick. Using a 3½-inch round cookie cutter, cut 9 circles from the dough. Place the circles of dough on the baking sheet. Prick several small holes over the entire surface of the dough circles with a fork, to prevent the dough from puffing too much. Transfer the puff pastry to the freezer to harden, about 10 minutes.

3 Cover the puff pastry with a sheet of parchment paper and then another flat baking sheet, to prevent the puff pastry from rising too much as it bakes. Bake for about 30 minutes. Carefully remove the top baking sheet and top layer of parchment and continue to bake for 5 to 10 more minutes, until crisp and deep golden brown. Let the puff pastry cool on the baking sheet.

Bread flour, for rolling

1 sheet (about 8 ounces) frozen puff pastry dough, thawed

36 Small Cream Puff Shells (page 34)

Vanilla Bean Pastry Cream (page 37)

2½ cups (500 grams) sugar

½ cup (120 grams) water

¼ cup plus 2 tablespoons (120 grams) light corn syrup

About 3 cups Whipped Cream (page 41)

Note *To avoid caramel burns, wear a pair of heat-resistant rubber dishwashing gloves while assembling your Gâteaux Saint-Honoré.*

4 **To assemble the gâteaux:** Place a round piping tip (such as Ateco #802) on the tip of your index finger, or use the tip of a paring knife, and pierce a ¼-inch hole in the bottom of each cream puff.

5 Fill a pastry bag fitted with the same round piping tip with the pastry cream. Piping into the hole in each cream puff, gently fill with pastry cream, taking care not to overfill. Set aside at room temperature until ready to use.

6 Prepare a large ice water bath. Line a baking sheet with parchment paper.

7 In a small saucepan, bring the sugar, water, and corn syrup to a boil, swirling the pan occasionally until the sugar has dissolved. Continue cooking until the caramel is light golden amber in color. Remove the pan from the heat, and plunge the bottom of the pan into the ice water bath to stop the cooking.

8 Very carefully dip the top of each of the filled cream puffs into the hot caramel, allowing any excess caramel to drip from the cream puff before inverting and setting aside on the prepared baking sheet. Let stand at room temperature until the caramel hardens, about 10 minutes. Set aside 9 of the cream puffs.

9 Very carefully dip the bottoms of the remaining 27 cream puffs, one by one, in the caramel, and then arrange them on the puff pastry circles in rings of 3, using the caramel to secure the cream puffs to the puff pastry. (If the caramel begins to harden before you are done, return the saucepan to the stovetop and reheat over medium heat until liquid.) Let the gâteaux stand at room temperature until the caramel cools and hardens, about 10 minutes.

10 Fill a pastry bag fitted with a star piping tip (such as Ateco #826) with the whipped cream and pipe 3 stripes of whipped cream between the cream puffs. Pipe a small rosette of cream on top of the gâteaux. Place one of the reserved cream puffs on the top of each rosette of cream. Serve immediately, or refrigerate for up to 1 day.

Note To clean the pot of caramel, fill with water and bring to a full boil. Continue to boil until the caramel dissolves completely.

French Crullers

MAKES 12 TO 14 CRULLERS

1 In a medium saucepan, bring the water, milk, butter, sugar, and salt to a rolling boil. Turn off the heat and add the flour all at once, while continuing to stir. Turn the heat to medium-low and cook the dough, while stirring constantly, until it forms a ball and leaves a skin on the base of the pot, 3 to 4 minutes.

2 Transfer the dough to a large bowl. Add the whole eggs, one at a time, stirring vigorously to combine between each addition. Scrape down the sides of the bowl with a rubber spatula as needed between each addition. Add the egg whites and mix the dough until the eggs are fully combined and the mixture is smooth. Fill a pastry bag fitted with a star piping tip (such as Ateco #826) with the dough and set aside at room temperature.

3 Cut out fourteen 3-inch squares of parchment paper and lightly coat them with nonstick cooking spray. Pipe a ring onto each square, about 2½ inches in diameter. Place the rings of

½ cup (120 grams) water

½ cup (120 grams) whole milk

6 tablespoons (84 grams) unsalted butter

1 tablespoon (13 grams) sugar

¼ teaspoon salt

1 cup (128 grams) unbleached all-purpose flour

3 large eggs

2 large egg whites

Nonstick cooking spray

Canola oil, for frying

French Cruller Glaze (page 72)

dough on a baking sheet and freeze until fully hardened, about 30 minutes, or until ready to fry.

4 **To fry the crullers:** Heat 2 inches of oil in a heavy pot to 375°F on an instant-read thermometer. Place a cooling rack over a baking sheet.

5 Carefully place one cruller at a time into the oil, paper side up. Gently remove the paper with tongs. Continue to add crullers to the oil, taking care to leave about 2 inches of space between each cruller. Fry the crullers until deep golden brown, 3 to 4 minutes on each side. Using a slotted spoon, carefully remove the crullers and set on the rack to cool. Once cool enough to handle, but still quite warm, dip the crullers into the glaze, on one or both sides, and return to the rack to cool completely. The crullers can be made 1 day ahead and stored in an airtight container at room temperature until ready to serve.

Note Save the original container the oil was purchased in and, once cooled to room temperature, pour it back into the container to store for reuse or disposal. You can reuse oil for frying two or three times before disposing of it. Simply strain the oil before reusing.

FRENCH CRULLER GLAZE

Sift the confectioners' sugar into a large bowl. Add the remaining ingredients and whisk by hand until smooth. The glaze should have the consistency of buttermilk, thick yet liquid. If the glaze needs to be thickened, slowly add confectioners' sugar until the glaze reaches the desired consistency. To thin the glaze, add milk or water, 1 tablespoon at a time. Cover the bowl with plastic wrap and set aside at room temperature until ready to use, up to 2 hours.

2¼ cups (270 grams) confectioners' sugar, plus more for adjusting glaze

4 tablespoons (56 grams) unsalted butter, melted

3 tablespoons (45 grams) water

2 tablespoons (30 grams) whole milk, plus more for adjusting glaze

1 teaspoon vanilla extract

¼ teaspoon salt

Seeds from 1 vanilla bean (optional)

Double Espresso Éclairs

1 Place a round piping tip (such as Ateco #802) on the tip of your index finger, or use the tip of a paring knife, and pierce two ¼-inch holes in the bottom of each éclair shell.

2 Fill a pastry bag fitted with the same round piping tip with the pastry cream. Piping into the holes in each éclair, gently fill with pastry cream.

3 Dip the top one-third of each éclair into the glaze, allowing the excess to drip away from the éclair before inverting. Sprinkle the tops of the éclairs with a few pinches of chopped coffee beans, if desired. Set aside until the glaze has fully set and hardened, about 20 minutes. As you are dipping the éclairs, adjust the thickness of the glaze as needed (see page 25). Serve immediately, or refrigerate for up to 8 hours.

16 to 18 Small Éclair Shells (page 31)

Espresso Pastry Cream (page 74)

Espresso Glaze (page 75)

Whole coffee beans, finely chopped, for decorating (optional)

Note Some of the filling recipes will produce more than needed for the amount of pâte à choux— this is because your pâte à choux puffs and éclairs may need more or less filling based on how much they puff while baking. If you end up with extra filling, just eat it by the spoonful!

ESPRESSO PASTRY CREAM

4 large egg yolks

1 large egg

¼ cup plus 3 tablespoons (53 grams) cornstarch

2 cups (480 grams) whole milk

½ cup plus 2 tablespoons (126 grams) sugar

¼ cup plus 1 tablespoon (20 grams) instant espresso powder

¼ teaspoon salt

5 tablespoons (70 grams) unsalted butter, cut into small pieces

1   In a large bowl, whisk the egg yolks, egg, and cornstarch together until completely smooth.

2   In a medium pot, bring the milk, sugar, espresso powder, and salt to a boil. Slowly pour the hot milk over the egg yolks while whisking constantly. Return the mixture to the pot and cook over medium-low heat, whisking constantly but slowly, until just thickened and bubbles rise to the surface, about 4 minutes. Increase the speed of whisking to smooth the custard and continue to cook until it has thickened to the consistency of pudding and coats the back of a spoon, about 2 more minutes.

3   Immediately remove the pot from the heat, add the butter, and whisk until fully melted and smooth. Strain the mixture through a fine-mesh sieve into a large bowl and cover the pastry cream with a sheet of plastic wrap directly on the surface to prevent a skin from forming. Refrigerate until cold and fully set, about 2 hours, or up to 3 days.

ESPRESSO GLAZE

Combine the water and espresso powder in a large bowl and stir until dissolved. Sift the confectioners' sugar over the espresso mixture. Add the corn syrup and salt and whisk until smooth. To make a thicker glaze, slowly add sifted confectioners' sugar until the glaze reaches the desired consistency. To make a thinner glaze, add water, 1 teaspoon at a time. Cover the bowl with plastic wrap and set aside at room temperature until ready to use, up to 1 day.

¼ cup (60 grams) warm water, plus more for adjusting glaze

3 tablespoons (12 grams) instant espresso powder

1½ cups (180 grams) confectioners' sugar, plus more for adjusting glaze

2 tablespoons (40 grams) light corn syrup

¼ teaspoon salt

Note The glaze should create a nearly opaque coating on the tops of the shells that are being glazed—thick enough so the shell is barely visible through the glaze, yet thin enough to allow for dipping with ease.

Croquembouche

1 Cover a 12-inch Styrofoam cone with parchment paper (the cone can be found at most craft supply stores) and place the cone on a parchment paper–lined baking sheet.

2 Place a round piping tip (such as Ateco #802) on the tip of your index finger, or use the tip of a paring knife, and pierce a ¼-inch hole in the bottom of each cream puff shell.

3 Fill a pastry bag fitted with the same round piping tip with the vanilla pastry cream. Piping into the hole in each of 24 of the cream puffs, gently fill with pastry cream. Fill another 24 cream puffs with the chocolate pastry cream, and then fill the last 24 cream puffs with the espresso pastry cream.

4 Divide the glaze into small bowls and color each portion with food colorings. If using sprinkles, glitter, or luster dust, color the glazes a shade or two lighter than the decorations. Cover the bowls of glaze with plastic wrap until ready to use.

72 Small Cream Puff Shells (page 34)

Vanilla Bean Pastry Cream (page 37)

Chocolate Pastry Cream (page 38)

Espresso Pastry Cream (page 74)

2 recipes White Glaze (page 40)

Assorted gel paste food coloring

Assorted colored sprinkles, edible glitters, and luster dusts, for decorating (optional)

Royal Icing (page 41)

Note The croquembouche is a classic French wedding cake. Be forewarned: This recipe is the absolute hardest in this book. The end result will have you feeling glorious, but it takes a lot of time, patience, and planning. Ask yourself, "Am I in the mood to make a wedding cake today?" If yes, go for it and don't look back!

5 Working with one color at a time, dip the top half of some of the cream puffs into one of the bowls of glaze, allowing the excess glaze to drip away from each cream puff before inverting. (For the croquembouche pictured, I used six colors, with 12 cream puffs in each color.) Set the glazed cream puffs aside for a few minutes to let the glaze begin to set. Decorate the cream puffs with sprinkles, glitter, or luster dust, if desired. Repeat with the remaining cream puffs and different colored glazes. Let the finished cream puffs stand at room temperature until the glaze has fully set, about 20 minutes.

6 Fill a pastry bag fitted with a coupler and a small piping tip (such as Ateco #5) with the royal icing.

7 **To assemble the croquembouche:** Pipe a ring of royal icing on the bottom of one of the cream puffs. Immediately press the cream puff against the cone at the very base, and hold in place until the icing allows the cream puff to adhere to the cone. Repeat with more cream puffs, working slowly and carefully, placing them in a ring at the base of the cone. Add more cream puffs in a second ring, just above and staggered slightly to the right of the first, taking care to arrange the puffs as close together as possible to hide the cone and create a tight pattern. If needed, rotate the cream puffs to find the sides that best fit together, much like jigsaw puzzle pieces. With each ring, fit the cream puffs between the two cream puffs arranged just below. If needed, pipe a small dot of icing on the sides of the cream puffs to help secure them to each other. Continue to attach the cream puffs until the entire cone is covered. Once the croquembouche is fully assembled, let it stand for 1 to 2 hours to allow the icing to fully set. Serve within 4 hours of assembling.

8   Reserve the remaining royal icing in the pastry bag, and press a toothpick into the piping tip to seal the bag from air so the icing won't dry out. If any of the puffs fall off the croquembouche, use the reserved icing to reattach.

Note Make your life easier and break this recipe into a multiday project. Bake the puffs on one day, up to 2 weeks in advance if you plan to freeze them. Make the pastry creams on another day, no more than 3 days before you plan to fill the puffs. Finish on the day you plan to serve the croquembouche by making the glazes, assembling, and decorating.

Fruity

Strawberry-Rhubarb Religieuses

⊶ MAKES ABOUT 18 RELIGIEUSES ⊷

1 Preheat the oven to 350°F. Line two baking sheets with parchment paper.

2 For the small cream puffs: Fit a pastry bag with a round piping tip (such as Ateco #806) and fill with two-thirds of the pâte à choux dough. Pipe 18 small mounds, about 1¼ inch in diameter and 1 inch tall, onto one of the baking sheets, leaving about 1 inch of space between each mound. Bake until deep golden brown and cooked through in the center, 40 to 45 minutes. Let cool on the baking sheet to room temperature.

3 For the miniature cream puffs: Fit a second pastry bag with a smaller round piping tip (such as Ateco #804) and fill with the remaining dough. Pipe 18 tiny mounds, about ¾ inch in diameter and ½ inch tall, on the other baking sheet, leaving about ½ inch of space between each mound. Bake for 35 to 40 minutes, until deep golden brown and

Pâte à Choux Dough (page 28)

Vanilla Bean Pastry Cream (page 37)

Strawberry-Rhubarb Jam (page 85), or 1 cup (about 225 grams) store-bought

White Glaze (page 40), tinted pink

Note Feel free to skip the pastry cream and go all jam. The recipe for the jam will make plenty to fill all the puffs in the recipe.

cooked through in the center. Let cool on the baking sheet to room temperature.

4   Place a round piping tip (such as Ateco #802) on the tip of your index finger, or use the tip of a paring knife, and pierce a ¼-inch hole in the bottom of each of the small and miniature cream puffs.

5   Fill a pastry bag fitted with the same round piping tip with the pastry cream. Fill a second pastry bag, fitted with another round piping tip (such as Ateco #802), with the jam. Piping into the holes on the bottom, gently fill each of the small cream puffs with the pastry cream. Gently fill each of the miniature cream puffs with the jam.

6   Dip the top one-third of both the small and miniature cream puffs into the glaze, allowing the excess to drip away from each cream puff before inverting. Set aside until the glaze has fully set and hardened, about 20 minutes. As you are dipping the cream puffs, adjust the thickness of the glaze as needed (see page 25).

7   **To assemble the religieuses:** Pipe a ¼-inch round dollop of pastry cream on the top of each small cream puff. Set a miniature cream puff on the pastry cream, pressing gently to stabilize. Decoratively pipe a small dot of pastry cream on the top of each religieuse. Serve immediately, or refrigerate for up to 8 hours.

STRAWBERRY-RHUBARB JAM

1 In a large pot, combine the rhubarb, strawberries, water, and vanilla seeds over medium heat and cook, stirring frequently, until the rhubarb is just tender, about 10 minutes.

2 Add the sugar and salt. Adjust the heat to low and cook, stirring occasionally, until the jam has just thickened, skimming off and discarding any foam that rises to the surface. Continue cooking until the jam reaches 220°F on an instant-read thermometer. Remove from the heat and stir in the lime juice. Let cool until cool enough to handle, then transfer the mixture to a blender and puree until smooth. Refrigerate, uncovered, until chilled and set, about 2 hours. If making ahead, store the jam in an airtight container in the refrigerator for up to 2 weeks.

1 pound (454 grams) rhubarb, fresh or frozen, sliced into ½-inch pieces

½ pound (227 grams) strawberries, hulled and chopped

½ cup (120 grams) water

Seeds from ½ vanilla bean

2½ cups (400 grams) sugar

¼ teaspoon salt

Juice of 1 lime

Note This jam recipe yields about three-quarters more than you will need to fill the religieuses. But it is so good that I suggest you follow the recipe as is, and enjoy the extra on toast or over vanilla ice cream.

Strawberry Shortcakes

MAKES 8 TO 10 SHORTCAKES

Using a serrated knife, slice the Paris-Brest shells in half horizontally, setting the tops next to their corresponding bottoms. Fill a pastry bag fitted with a star piping tip (such as Ateco #827) with the whipped cream and pipe rings on the Paris-Brest bases. Cover the whipped cream with an even layer of strawberry slices, then gently set the tops of the Paris-Brest shells on the fruit. Serve immediately, or refrigerate for up to 8 hours.

8 to 10 Paris-Brest Shells (page 36)

Lemon Whipped Cream (recipe follows)

½ pound (227 grams) strawberries, hulled and thinly sliced

LEMON WHIPPED CREAM

MAKES ABOUT 3 CUPS

By hand or using a stand mixer fitted with the whisk attachment, whip the cream, confectioners' sugar, and lemon zest until stiff peaks form. Cover and refrigerate until ready to use, up to 2 hours. If the cream softens while sitting in the refrigerator, re-whip until stiff peaks form before using.

1½ cups (360 grams) heavy whipping cream

¼ cup plus 2 tablespoons (44 grams) confectioners' sugar, sifted

Finely grated zest of ½ lemon

Strawberry Shortcakes and Peaches and Cream Puffs (page 88) ▶

Peaches and Cream Puffs

1 Fill a pastry bag fitted with a round piping tip (such as Ateco #804) with the whipped cream and refrigerate until ready to use. Halve, pit, and cut the peaches into ⅛-inch slices. Using a serrated knife, slice the cream puff shells in half lengthwise and arrange the tops and bottoms side by side until ready to glaze and fill.

2 Dip the top of each cream puff into the glaze, allowing the excess to drip away from the cream puff before inverting. As you are dipping the cream puffs, adjust the thickness of the glaze as needed (see page 25).

3 Spread about 2 teaspoons of the peach preserves on the bottom of each puff. Pipe the whipped cream in spirals over the preserves, filling each puff about 1 inch high. Fan a few peach slices over the filling. Set the peach-glazed tops on top. Refrigerate the puffs for about 30 minutes to allow the filling to set before serving, or for up to 8 hours.

Whipped Cream (page 41)

3 ripe peaches

14 to 16 Large Cream Puff Shells (page 35)

Fresh Peach Glaze (page 89)

1 cup (about 300 grams) good-quality peach preserves

Note If you find yourself at the farmers' market and the summer nectarines or plums look better than the peaches, use them instead! There's no need to follow a recipe such as this exactly. . . .

FRESH PEACH GLAZE

Halve, pit, and chop the peach. Puree the peach and honey in a blender until completely smooth. Sift the confectioners' sugar into a medium bowl. Add the peach puree and salt and whisk until smooth. The glaze should have a thick consistency that still allows for dipping. To make a thicker glaze, slowly add sifted confectioners' sugar until the glaze reaches the desired consistency. To make a thinner glaze, add water, 1 teaspoon at a time. Cover the bowl with plastic wrap and set aside at room temperature until ready to use, up to 2 hours.

½ **ripe peach**

1 **tablespoon (20 grams) honey**

1½ **cups (180 grams) confectioners' sugar, plus more for adjusting glaze**

¼ **teaspoon salt**

Fruity Pâte à Choux Pops

MAKES 30 TO 36 PÂTE À CHOUX POPS

1   Place a round piping tip (such as Ateco #802) on the tip of your index finger, or use the tip of a paring knife, and pierce a ¼-inch hole in the bottom of each cream puff shell.

2   Fill a pastry bag fitted with the same round piping tip with the pastry cream. Fill another pastry bag, fitted with another round piping tip, with the preserves. Piping into the holes on the bottom, fill each cream puff about halfway with the preserves. (If you plan to make more than one flavor of fruity pops, pipe different flavors of jam into the cream puffs.) Then fill each cream puff with the pastry cream until full.

3   Dip the top half of each cream puff into the glaze, allowing the excess glaze to drip away from the cream puff before inverting. Decorate the cream puffs with luster dusts. Let the cream puffs stand at room temperature until the glaze has fully set, about 20 minutes. Place a lollipop stick into each of the puffs, using the hole previously made for filling the puffs, and serve immediately, or refrigerate for up to 8 hours.

30 to 36 Small Cream Puff Shells (page 34)

Vanilla Bean Pastry Cream (page 37)

1½ cups (about 340 grams) store-bought fruit preserves, such as cherry, strawberry, or black raspberry

White Glaze (page 40), tinted to desired colors

Assorted luster dusts, for decorating

Note It's much easier to store the pops without their sticks. If you plan to make them in advance, pop the sticks into the puffs just before serving.

Peanut Butter and Jelly Éclairs

Using a serrated knife, cut each éclair shell in half lengthwise. Spread the top halves with some of the peanut butter and spread the bottom halves with grape jelly. Sprinkle the peanut butter with chopped peanuts, if desired. Press the tops and bottoms together to create a sandwich. Serve immediately.

Note *This is an incredibly kid-friendly recipe to make and eat. Of course, we Americans love our grape jelly, but you can certainly swap it for any jelly or jam you love best.*

10 to 12 Large Éclair Shells (page 33)

1 (16-ounce) jar (about 450 grams) creamy peanut butter

1 cup (about 300 grams) Concord grape jelly

Roasted peanuts, finely chopped, for sprinkling (optional)

Blueberry Cheesecake Gâteaux Saint-Honoré

>○ MAKES 9 INDIVIDUAL GÂTEAUX ○<

1 Preheat the oven to 375°F. Line a baking sheet with parchment paper.

2 On a lightly floured surface, roll the puff pastry to ⅛ inch thick. Using a 3½-inch round cookie cutter, cut 9 circles from the dough and then place them on the baking sheet. Prick several small holes over the entire surface of the dough circles with a fork, to prevent the dough from rising too much. Transfer the dough to the freezer to harden, about 10 minutes.

3 Remove the baking sheet from the freezer and cover with a sheet of parchment paper and another flat baking sheet, to prevent the puff pastry from rising too much as it bakes. Bake the pastry for about 30 minutes. Carefully remove the top baking sheet and top layer of parchment paper and continue to bake for about 5 more minutes, until crisp and deep golden brown. Let the puff pastry cool on the baking sheet.

Bread flour, for rolling

1 sheet (about 8 ounces) frozen puff pastry dough, thawed

36 Small Cream Puff Shells (page 34)

3 cups (about 680 grams) blueberry jam

White Glaze (page 40), tinted blue

Whipped Cream Cheese (page 97)

Blueberries, for decorating

Note Several recipes call for store-bought jams and jellies in this book. That's because they are yummy and easy to use, especially for recipes that already require several made-from-scratch components. If you are extra adventurous, you can always make them homemade.

◀ *Blueberry Cheesecake Gâteaux Saint-Honoré and Citrus Gâteaux Saint-Honoré (page 98)*

4   To assemble the gâteaux: Place a round piping tip (such as Ateco #802) on the tip of your index finger, or use the tip of a paring knife, and pierce a ¼-inch hole in the bottom of each cream puff shell.

5   Fill a pastry bag fitted with the same round piping tip with the blueberry jam. Piping into the hole in each cream puff, gently fill with jam, taking care not to overfill. Set aside at room temperature until ready to use.

6   Dip the top of each cream puff into the glaze and set aside until the glaze has fully set and hardened, about 20 minutes. Set aside 9 of the cream puffs.

7   Dip the bottoms of the remaining 27 cream puffs, one by one, into the glaze, and then arrange them on the puff pastry in rings of 3, using the glaze to secure the cream puffs to the puff pastry. Let the cream puffs stand at room temperature until the glaze hardens, about 20 minutes.

8   Fill a pastry bag fitted with a star piping tip (such as Ateco #826) with the whipped cream cheese and pipe 3 stripes of whipped cream cheese between the cream puffs. Pipe a small rosette on top of the gâteaux, and then place one of the reserved cream puffs on the top. Garnish each gâteau with a few blueberries. Serve immediately, or store in the refrigerator for up to 1 day.

WHIPPED CREAM CHEESE

In the bowl of a stand mixer fitted with the whisk attachment, whip the cream and cream cheese on medium speed until just smooth. Reduce the speed to low, slowly add the confectioners' sugar, vanilla, and lemon juice and continue to mix until combined. Scrape down the sides of the bowl, raise the mixer speed to high, and beat until thickened and stiff peaks form, about 1 minute. Set aside in the refrigerator until ready to use, up to 4 hours.

1 cup (240 grams) heavy whipping cream

1 cup (225 grams) cream cheese, softened

¼ cup (30 grams) confectioners' sugar, sifted

1 teaspoon vanilla extract

Juice of ½ lemon

Citrus Gâteaux Saint-Honoré

1 Preheat the oven to 375°F. Line a baking sheet with parchment paper.

2 On a lightly floured surface, roll the puff pastry to ⅛ inch thick. Using a 3½-inch round cookie cutter, cut 9 circles from the dough. Place the circles of dough on the baking sheet. Prick several small holes over the entire surface area of the dough circles with a fork to prevent the dough from rising too much. Transfer the baking sheet with the dough circles to the freezer to harden, about 15 minutes.

3 Remove the dough from the freezer and cover with a sheet of parchment paper and then another flat baking sheet, to prevent the puff pastry from rising too much as it bakes. Bake for about 30 minutes. Carefully remove the top baking sheet and top layer of parchment paper and continue to bake the puff pastry for about 5 more minutes, until crisp and deep golden brown. Let the puff pastry cool on the baking sheet to room temperature.

Bread flour, for rolling

1 sheet (about 8 ounces) frozen puff pastry dough, thawed

36 Small Cream Puff Shells (page 34)

Lemon Curd (page 112)

White Glaze (page 40), tinted lime green

Yellow and white nonpareils, for decorating (optional)

Lime Whipped Cream (page 100)

Note To save yourself a bit of kitchen labor, you can buy a jar of good-quality lemon curd instead of making it from scratch. I promise I won't judge you.

4 To assemble the gâteaux: Place a round piping tip (such as Ateco #802) on the tip of your index finger, or use the tip of a paring knife, and pierce a ¼-inch hole in the bottom of each cream puff shell.

5 Fill a pastry bag fitted with the same round piping tip with the lemon curd. Piping into the hole in each cream puff, gently fill with lemon curd, taking care not to overfill. Set aside at room temperature until ready to use.

6 Dip the top of each cream puff into the glaze. Decorate with nonpareils, if desired. Set aside until the glaze has fully set and hardened, about 20 minutes. As you are dipping the cream puffs, adjust the thickness of the glaze as needed (see page 25). Set aside 9 of the glazed cream puffs.

7 Dip the bottoms of the remaining 27 cream puffs into the glaze, and arrange them on the puff pastry circles in rings of 3, using the glaze to secure them to the puff pastry. Let stand at room temperature until the glaze hardens, about 20 minutes.

8 Fill a pastry bag fitted with a star piping tip (such as Ateco #826) with the whipped cream and pipe 3 stripes of whipped cream between the cream puffs. Pipe a small rosette of whipped cream on top of the gâteaux and then place one of the reserved cream puffs on the top. Serve immediately, or refrigerate for up to 1 day.

LIME WHIPPED CREAM

By hand or using a stand mixer fitted with the whisk attachment, whip the cream, confectioners' sugar, and lime zest until soft peaks form. Add the lime juice and continue to whip until stiff peaks form. Cover and refrigerate until ready to use, up to 2 hours. If the cream softens while sitting in the refrigerator, re-whip until stiff peaks form before using.

2 cups (480 grams) heavy whipping cream

¼ cup (30 grams) confectioners' sugar, sifted

Finely grated zest of 2 limes

Juice of 2 limes

Melon, Mint, and Yogurt Mousse Éclairs

1   Using a serrated knife, trim off the top one-third of each éclair shell lengthwise and discard the tops.

2   Using various size melon ballers, ranging in size from ¼ to ½ inch in diameter, scoop an assortment of balls from the honeydew and cantaloupe.

3   Fill a pastry bag fitted with a round piping tip (such as Ateco #803) with the mousse. Pipe dots of mousse onto the base of each éclair to fill. Set the melon balls on top of the filling to create an irregular dotted pattern, leaving some of the filling exposed. Tear the mint leaves into very small pieces and garnish each éclair with the mint. Serve immediately.

10 to 12 Large Éclair Shells (page 33)

½ ripe honeydew melon, seeds removed

½ ripe cantaloupe, seeds removed

Yogurt Mousse (page 103)

Leaves from 3 or 4 sprigs fresh mint

YOGURT MOUSSE

1 Place the yogurt in a large bowl.

2 Sprinkle the gelatin over the milk in a small
   pot and let stand for 1 minute to soften. Add
   the sugar, honey, and salt and gently warm to
   a simmer over low heat, stirring until the sugar
   and gelatin are dissolved. Strain the mixture
   through a fine-mesh sieve over the yogurt and
   whisk until smooth.

3 By hand or using a stand mixer fitted with the
   whisk attachment, whip the cream until stiff
   peaks form. Gently fold the whipped cream
   into the yogurt mixture, using a whisk, and
   refrigerate until thickened, about 2 hours.

*Note Prefer a little less time in the kitchen?
Skip making the mousse and fill the éclairs with
plain Greek yogurt. Add a little sugar to the
yogurt to sweeten it before using.*

1 cup (225 grams) whole-milk
yogurt

1 teaspoon powdered gelatin

⅓ cup (80 grams) whole milk

1 tablespoon (13 grams)
granulated sugar

2 tablespoons (40 grams) honey

¼ teaspoon salt

½ cup (120 grams) heavy
whipping cream

◀ *Clockwise from top left: Mango-Pineapple Éclairs (page 104); Melon, Mint,
and Yogurt Mousse Éclairs; and Jasmine-Pomegranate Éclairs (page 106)*

Mango-Pineapple Éclairs

1 Peel and core the pineapple and cut into wedge-shaped spears about ½ inch wide. Cut the spears into thin slices about ⅛ inch thick.

2 Using a serrated knife, trim off the top one-third of each éclair shell lengthwise and discard the tops. Spread the mousse in the base of each éclair until filled just to the top. Lay several pineapple slices of on top of the mousse. Sprinkle each éclair with a pinch of sea salt. Decorate with gold dragées, if desired. Serve immediately, or store in the refrigerator for up to 8 hours.

¼ to ½ ripe pineapple

16 to 18 Small Éclair Shells (page 31)

Mango Mousse (page 105)

Fine sea salt, for garnish

Gold dragées, for decorating (optional)

MANGO MOUSSE

MAKES ABOUT 1¼ CUPS

1   Peel, pit, and cut the mango into small chunks.
    Transfer the mango to a blender or food
    processor, add 2 tablespoons of the water,
    and puree until smooth. Measure 1 cup (about
    275 grams) of the mango puree and reserve.
    In a small bowl, sprinkle the gelatin over the
    remaining 1 tablespoon water and let it soften.

2   In a medium saucepan, bring the reserved
    mango puree and the sugar to a simmer.
    Remove from the heat, add the gelatin mixture,
    and stir until completely dissolved. Transfer
    the fruit puree to a large bowl and let it cool to
    room temperature.

3   By hand or using a stand mixer fitted with the
    whisk attachment, whip the cream until stiff
    peaks form. Carefully fold the whipped cream
    into the cooled fruit puree. Refrigerate until
    ready to use, up to 4 hours.

1 large ripe mango

3 tablespoons (45 grams) water

1 teaspoon powdered gelatin

**2 tablespoons (26 grams)
granulated sugar**

**½ cup (120 grams) heavy
whipping cream**

Jasmine-Pomegranate Éclairs

✄ MAKES 10 TO 12 LARGE ÉCLAIRS ✄

1 Using a serrated knife, trim off the top one-third of each éclair shell lengthwise and discard the tops.

2 Cut the pomegranates in half lengthwise. In a bowl of cold water to prevent juice from spraying, use your hands to separate the seeds from the membrane. Reserve the seeds and discard the membrane. Drain the seeds and pat dry. Refrigerate until ready to use.

3 Just before serving, spread the whipped cream in the base of each éclair until filled just to the top. Generously sprinkle the pomegranate seeds on top. Decorate with pink dragées, if desired. Serve immediately.

10 to 12 Large Éclair Shells (page 33)

2 large pomegranates

Jasmine Whipped Cream (page 107)

Light pink dragées, for decorating (optional)

Note *Purchasing prepared pomegranate seeds will save you time in this recipe. However, the flavor of freshly seeded pomegranate is far superior.*

JASMINE WHIPPED CREAM

By hand or using a stand mixer fitted with the whisk attachment, whip the cream and confectioners' sugar until soft peaks form. Add the jasmine extract and vanilla seeds, and continue to whip until stiff peaks form. Cover and refrigerate until ready to use, up to 2 hours. If the cream softens while sitting in the refrigerator, re-whip until stiff peaks form before using.

Note *My favorite source for jasmine extract is ChefRubber.com, but it can also be found in natural foods or beauty supply stores that sell flower extracts and essential oils.*

1 cup (240 grams) heavy whipping cream

¼ cup (30 grams) confectioners' sugar, sifted

1 teaspoon jasmine extract, or to taste

Seeds from 1 vanilla bean

Banana Pudding Puffs

MAKES 14 TO 16 LARGE CREAM PUFFS

1   Fill a pastry bag fitted with a round piping tip (such as Ateco #802) with the banana pudding and refrigerate until ready to use. Using a serrated knife, slice the cream puff shells in half lengthwise.

2   Dip the top of each cream puff into the glaze, allowing the excess to drip away before inverting. As you are dipping, adjust the thickness of the glaze as needed (see page 25).

3   Pipe the banana pudding in spirals over the bases of the cream puffs, filling each puff about 1 inch high. Set the glazed tops over the filling.

4   Peel the bananas and cut them into ¼-inch-thick slices. Place on a baking sheet or a piece of aluminum foil. Generously dust the top of each banana slice with the turbinado sugar. Using a handheld kitchen torch, caramelize the sugar to a light golden brown. Let cool to room temperature before using.

Banana Pudding Filling (page 110)

14 to 16 Large Cream Puff Shells (page 35)

White Glaze (page 40), tinted yellow

2 ripe bananas

Turbinado sugar, for caramelizing bananas

Note To caramelize the banana slices without a torch, place the banana slices, topped with turbinado sugar, on a baking sheet. Broil on low just until the sugar melts and becomes golden.

Banana Pudding Puffs and Lemon Meringue Pie Éclairs (page 111) ▶

5 Pipe a ¼-inch round dollop of pudding on the top of each cream puff, then set a caramelized banana slice on top for decoration, pressing gently to stabilize. Serve immediately.

BANANA PUDDING FILLING

MAKES ABOUT 3 CUPS

1 Peel and chop the bananas and puree until smooth in a blender or food processor.

2 In a large bowl, whisk the egg yolks, egg, and cornstarch until completely smooth.

3 In a medium pot, bring the pureed bananas, milk, sugar, salt, and vanilla seeds to a boil. Slowly pour the hot milk over the egg yolks while whisking constantly. Return the mixture to the pot and cook over medium-low heat, whisking constantly but slowly, until thickened and bubbles rise to the surface, 5 to 6 minutes.

4 Immediately remove the pot from the heat, add the butter, and whisk until fully melted and smooth. Strain the mixture through a fine-mesh sieve into a large bowl and cover the pudding with a sheet of plastic wrap directly on the surface to prevent a skin from forming. Refrigerate until cold and fully set, about 2 hours, or up to 2 days.

3 very ripe bananas

4 large egg yolks

1 large egg

¼ cup plus 3 tablespoons (53 grams) cornstarch

1¾ cups (420 grams) whole milk

½ cup plus 2 tablespoons (126 grams) sugar

¼ teaspoon salt

Seeds from 1 vanilla bean (optional)

5 tablespoons (70 grams) unsalted butter, cut into small pieces

Lemon Meringue Pie Éclairs

1 Fill a pastry bag fitted with a round piping tip (such as Ateco #805) with the meringue and refrigerate until ready to use.

2 Using a serrated knife, cut off the top one-third of each éclair lengthwise and discard the tops. Spread the lemon curd into each éclair shell, filling just over the top. Decoratively pipe three large drops of meringue on top of the lemon curd. Serve immediately, or refrigerate for up to 8 hours.

Italian Meringue (page 113)

16 to 18 Small Éclair Shells (page 31)

Lemon Curd (page 112)

LEMON CURD

1 Bring a medium pot filled with about 2 inches of water to a simmer.

2 In a large heatproof bowl, whisk the sugar, lemon zest and juice, egg yolks, eggs, and salt together until evenly combined. Place the bowl over the simmering water and, while whisking constantly, cook the curd until the mixture thickens and reaches 165°F on an instant-read thermometer, 10 to 12 minutes.

3 Immediately remove the curd from the heat, add the butter, and whisk until fully melted and smooth. Strain the mixture through a fine-mesh sieve into a large bowl and cover the curd with a sheet of plastic wrap directly on the surface to prevent a skin from forming. Refrigerate until cold and fully set, about 2 hours, or up to 1 week.

¾ cup (150 grams) sugar

Finely grated zest of 4 lemons

1 cup (240 grams) freshly squeezed lemon juice (from about 8 lemons)

8 large egg yolks

3 large eggs

¼ teaspoon salt

2 sticks (226 grams) unsalted butter, cut into small pieces

ITALIAN MERINGUE

MAKES ABOUT 3 CUPS

1 In the bowl of a stand mixer fitted with the whisk attachment, whip the egg whites on low speed.

2 Meanwhile, combine the sugar, water, honey, and salt in a small saucepan and cook over medium heat until the mixture reaches 238°F on an instant-read thermometer, about 12 minutes.

3 Immediately remove from the heat, increase the speed of the mixer to medium-high, and very slowly pour the hot sugar mixture over the egg whites, taking care not to pour the hot mixture onto the moving whisk.

4 Raise the speed of the mixer to high and whip until tripled in volume, thick, glossy, and cooled to room temperature, about 10 minutes. Refrigerate until ready to use, up to 4 hours (or freeze in an airtight container for up to 1 week).

3 large egg whites

1 cup (200 grams) sugar

½ cup (120 grams) water

1 tablespoon (20 grams) honey

¼ teaspoon salt

Note Lemon curd stores easily in the refrigerator for up to a week. And Italian meringue can be stored in the freezer for up to a week. So if you like a midnight sweet, you can do what I do—assemble an éclair or two each night for a week when no one is looking.

Pistachio–Black Mission Fig Éclairs

Using a serrated knife, cut off the top one-third of each éclair shell lengthwise and discard. Spread the pastry cream into the bottom of each éclair until just full. Fill a pastry bag fitted with a petal piping tip (such as Ateco #104) with the remaining pastry cream. Decoratively pipe the pastry cream in a zigzag pattern over the top of each éclair. Decorate with the quartered fig. Serve immediately, or refrigerate for up to 8 hours.

10 to 12 Large Éclair Shells (page 33)

Pistachio Pastry Cream (page 116)

12 large Black Mission figs, cut into quarters

Note If fresh Black Mission figs are out of season, simply substitute sliced dried figs to make these treats any time of the year.

◀ *Apple Butter Bombs (page 117) and Pistachio–Black Mission Fig Éclairs*

PISTACHIO PASTRY CREAM

MAKES ABOUT 3 CUPS

1 In a large bowl, whisk the egg yolks, egg, and cornstarch until completely smooth.

2 In a medium pot, bring the milk, sugar, and salt to a boil. Slowly pour the hot milk over the egg mixture while whisking constantly. Return the mixture to the pot and cook over medium-low heat, whisking constantly but slowly, until just thickened and bubbles rise to the surface, about 4 minutes. Increase the speed of whisking to smooth the custard and continue to cook until it has thickened to the consistency of pudding and coats the back of a spoon, about 2 more minutes.

3 Immediately remove the pot from the heat, add the pistachio paste and butter, and whisk until fully melted and smooth. Strain the mixture through a fine-mesh sieve into a large bowl and cover the pastry cream with a sheet of plastic wrap directly on the surface to prevent a skin from forming. Refrigerate until cold and fully set, about 2 hours, or up to 3 days.

4 large egg yolks

1 large egg

¼ cup plus 2 tablespoons (45 grams) cornstarch

2 cups (480 grams) whole milk

½ cup plus 2 tablespoons (126 grams) sugar

¼ teaspoon salt

½ cup (150 grams) pistachio paste or pistachio butter

5 tablespoons (70 grams) unsalted butter, cut into small pieces

Apple Butter Bombs

1 Place a round piping tip (such as Ateco #802) on the tip of your index finger, or use the tip of a paring knife, and pierce a ¼-inch hole in the bottom of each cream puff shell.

2 Fill a pastry bag fitted with the same round piping tip with the pastry cream. Fill another pastry bag, fitted with another round piping tip, with the apple butter. Piping into the hole in each cream puff, gently fill with the apple butter until one-third full. Then gently fill each cream puff with the pastry cream until full. Dust with confectioners' sugar and serve immediately, or refrigerate for up to 8 hours.

14 to 16 Large Cream Puff Shells (page 35)

Vanilla Bean Pastry Cream (page 37)

1½ cups (340 grams) store-bought apple butter

Confectioners' sugar, for dusting

Note Not enough time to make pastry cream? You can buy store-bought vanilla pudding instead, or fill these bombs with only apple butter.

Chocolate

Whoopie Puffs

1 Preheat the oven to 350°F. Line two baking sheets with parchment paper.

2 Fill a pastry bag fitted with a round piping tip (such as Ateco #806) with the pâte à choux dough and pipe 28 small disks (you'll have 4 extra, for any mishaps or for snacking), about 1½ inches in diameter and ½ inch thick, on the baking sheets, leaving about 1 inch of space between each disk. Lightly moisten a fingertip with cold water and gently smooth any peaks or points created when piping. Bake for 35 to 40 minutes, until cooked through in the center. Let cool on the baking sheets to room temperature.

3 **To flavor the buttercream:** Grind the freeze-dried raspberries to a fine powder in a food processor. Grind the pistachios to a fine powder.

Cocoa Pâte à Choux Dough (page 29)

¼ cup (12 grams) freeze-dried raspberries

2 tablespoons (18 grams) roasted pistachios

Swiss Meringue Buttercream (page 123)

1 tablespoon (8 grams) cocoa powder, sifted

1 to 2 teaspoons ground cinnamon

Finely grated zest of 1 lemon

Seeds from ½ vanilla bean

4 Divide the buttercream into six small bowls. Fold the freeze-dried raspberry powder, ground pistachios, cocoa powder, cinnamon, lemon zest, and vanilla seeds into each of the small bowls of buttercream until well combined and smooth.

5 Using a serrated knife, cut the pâte à choux disks in half horizontally. Spread a generous dollop of buttercream on the base of each disk, enough so the filling spills slightly over the sides, dividing the different buttercream flavors onto 4 disks each. Gently set the tops of the disks on the buttercream to create sandwiches, and smooth the sides of the buttercream with a spatula if needed. Serve immediately, or refrigerate for up to 1 day.

Note If making several flavors of buttercream filling feels way too complicated, make your life easy and just pick your favorite flavor or two. Good bakers always know their limits.

SWISS MERINGUE BUTTERCREAM

1 Cut the butter into small pieces.

2 Place the egg whites, sugar, and salt in the bowl of a stand mixer. Place the bowl over a saucepan filled with about 2 inches of simmering water and whisk constantly until the sugar is dissolved and the bowl is warm to the touch. Transfer the mixture to the base of the stand mixer, fitted with the whisk attachment, and whip the egg-white mixture on high speed until thick, glossy, and cooled to room temperature.

3 Reduce the speed of the mixer to low and slowly add the softened butter, one piece at a time. Scrape down the sides of the bowl, raise the mixer speed to high, and whip until thickened and completely smooth, about 5 minutes. Let stand at room temperature until ready to use.

3 sticks (336 grams) unsalted butter, softened

4 large egg whites

⅔ cup (133 grams) sugar

¼ teaspoon salt

Note Buttercream can be made up to 5 days in advance and refrigerated until ready to use. Let the buttercream stand at room temperature until softened. If the texture is not smooth, re-whip in the mixer until lightened and fluffy. This can take up to 10 minutes.

▲ *Passion Fruit–Chocolate Éclairs (page 128) and White Chocolate–Yuzu Éclairs*

White Chocolate–Yuzu Éclairs

$\circ\!\!\!\!\!\!<$ MAKES 16 TO 18 SMALL ÉCLAIRS $>\!\!\!\!\!\!\circ$

1 Place a round piping tip (such as Ateco #802) on the tip of your index finger, or use the tip of a paring knife, and pierce two ¼-inch holes in the bottom of each éclair shell.

2 Fill a pastry bag fitted with the same round piping tip with the mousse. Piping into the holes in each éclair, gently fill with mousse. Set the éclairs aside in the refrigerator until ready to glaze.

3 Dip the top one-third of each éclair into the glaze, allowing the excess to drip away from the éclair before inverting. Decorate with lime zest, if desired. Set aside until the glaze has fully set and hardened, about 20 minutes. As you are dipping the éclairs, adjust the thickness of the glaze as needed (see page 25).

16 to 18 Small Éclair Shells (page 31)

White Chocolate–Yuzu Mousse (page 126)

Yuzu Glaze (page 127)

Lime zest, for decorating (optional)

Note Yuzu juice can usually be found in the refrigerator case at a Japanese grocery store or a grocery store with a large selection of specialty ingredients.

WHITE CHOCOLATE–YUZU MOUSSE

1 In the bowl of a stand mixer fitted with the whisk attachment, whip the cream until soft peaks form. Transfer to a large bowl and refrigerate until ready to use.

2 In a heatproof bowl set over a pot of simmering water, melt the white chocolate. Remove from the heat and let stand at room temperature until ready to use.

3 In the clean bowl of the stand mixer, fitted with the whisk attachment, beat the egg yolks on medium speed. Meanwhile, in a small pot, cook the sugar, water, corn syrup, and salt until the mixture reaches 220°F on an instant-read thermometer. Immediately remove the pot from the heat and slowly pour over the egg yolks, with the mixer running, taking care not to pour the hot mixture onto the moving whisk. Add the gelatin and mix until combined. Raise the mixer speed to high and whip until light, fluffy, and cooled to room temperature.

¾ cup (180 grams) heavy whipping cream

1¼ cups (213 grams) white chocolate, chopped or chips

3 large egg yolks

3 tablespoons (39 grams) sugar

2 tablespoons (30 grams) water

1 tablespoon (20 grams) light corn syrup

¼ teaspoon salt

1 teaspoon powdered gelatin

2 tablespoons (28 grams) yuzu juice

Note *If you would prefer to use a more common ingredient, grapefruit juice is a fine substitute. Use it in place of the yuzu juice, and add the zest of ½ grapefruit, too.*

4 Remove the bowl of whipped egg yolks from the mixer, add the melted chocolate, and quickly fold until smooth. Fold one-quarter of the whipped cream into the mousse until combined. Add the remaining whipped cream and gently fold until smooth. Add the yuzu juice and fold until evenly incorporated. Use immediately, or refrigerate until ready to use, up to 4 hours.

YUZU GLAZE

MAKES ABOUT ¾ CUP

Sift the confectioners' sugar into a large bowl. Add the remaining ingredients and whisk by hand until smooth. The glaze should have a thick consistency that still allows for dipping. To make a thicker glaze, slowly add sifted confectioners' sugar until the glaze reaches the desired consistency. To make a thinner glaze, add yuzu juice, 1 teaspoon at a time. Cover the bowl with plastic wrap and set aside at room temperature until ready to use.

1½ cups (180 grams) confectioners' sugar, plus more for adjusting glaze

2 tablespoons (40 grams) light corn syrup

2 tablespoons (28 grams) yuzu juice, plus more for adjusting glaze

¼ teaspoon salt

Passion Fruit–Chocolate Éclairs

1 Place a round piping tip (such as Ateco #802) on the tip of your index finger, or use the tip of a paring knife, and pierce three ¼-inch holes in the bottom of each éclair shell.

2 Fill a pastry bag fitted with the same round piping tip with the passion fruit curd. Piping into the holes in each éclair, gently fill with passion fruit curd.

3 Dip the top one-third of each éclair into the glaze, allowing the excess to drip away from the éclair before inverting. Sprinkle with chopped chocolate, if desired. Set aside until the glaze has fully set and hardened, about 20 minutes. As you are dipping the éclairs, adjust the thickness of the glaze as needed (see page 25). Serve immediately, or refrigerate for up to 8 hours.

10 to 12 Large Éclair Shells (page 33)

Passion Fruit Curd (page 129)

Chocolate Glaze (page 39)

Bittersweet chocolate, finely chopped, for decorating (optional)

PASSION FRUIT CURD

1 Bring a medium pot filled with about 2 inches of water to a simmer.

2 In a large heatproof bowl, whisk the sugar, passion fruit puree, egg yolks, eggs, and salt until evenly combined. Place the bowl over the simmering water and, while whisking constantly, cook the curd until it reaches 165°F on an instant-read thermometer or the mixture just begins to thicken, 10 to 12 minutes.

3 Immediately remove the curd from the heat, add the butter, and whisk until fully melted and smooth. Strain the mixture through a fine-mesh sieve into a large bowl and cover the curd with a sheet of plastic wrap directly on the surface to prevent a skin from forming. Refrigerate until cold and fully set, about 2 hours, or up to 5 days.

½ cup (100 grams) sugar

½ cup (125 grams) frozen passion fruit puree, thawed

4 large egg yolks

2 large eggs

¼ teaspoon salt

1 stick (112 grams) unsalted butter, cut into small pieces

Note Frozen passion fruit puree can be found at most grocery stores that specialize in Latin foods. However, if your grocery store doesn't carry it, but they do carry Goya brand products, don't hesitate to ask the buyer to special-order the puree for you. You'd be surprised at how happily they will accommodate.

Chocolate Truffles

1 Place a round piping tip (such as Ateco #802) on the tip of your index finger, or use the tip of a paring knife, and pierce a ¼-inch hole in the bottom of each cream puff shell. Sift the cocoa powder into a shallow dish or bowl. Place the pistachios and coconut in separate shallow dishes or bowls.

2 Melt the chocolate in a heatproof bowl set over a pot of simmering water. Once melted, turn off the heat and keep warm until ready to use.

3 Fill a pastry bag fitted with the same round piping tip with the chocolate mousse. Piping into the hole in each cream puff, gently fill with mousse. Wipe away any excess mousse from the exterior of the cream puffs. Drop 2 or 3 filled cream puffs into the melted chocolate and, using a fork, roll them around in the chocolate until completely coated. Using the fork, remove the coated cream puffs from the melted chocolate, allowing excess chocolate to drip away. Drop the coated cream puffs into the cocoa powder, pistachios, or coconut and,

30 to 36 Small Cream Puff Shells (page 34)

Cocoa powder, for coating

Pistachios, finely ground, for coating

Unsweetened shredded coconut, for coating

2 cups (340 grams) bittersweet chocolate, chopped or chips

Bittersweet Chocolate Mousse (page 132)

using a separate fork for each, gently roll the cream puff to coat. Transfer the coated truffles to a rack and let sit until the chocolate coating has hardened, about 15 minutes. Transfer the truffles to a plate or baking sheet and refrigerate until set, about 15 minutes or up to 4 hours. Just before serving, let the truffles warm slightly at room temperature for about 15 minutes. Truffles are best eaten immediately.

BITTERSWEET CHOCOLATE MOUSSE

MAKES ABOUT 3 CUPS

1   In the bowl of a stand mixer fitted with the whisk attachment, whip the cream until soft peaks form. Transfer to another bowl and set aside at room temperature until ready to use.

2   In a heatproof bowl, set over a pot of simmering water, melt the chocolate. Remove from the heat and let stand at room temperature until ready to use.

3   In the clean bowl of the stand mixer, fitted with the whisk attachment, whip the egg yolks on medium speed. Meanwhile, in a small pot, cook the sugar, water, corn syrup, vanilla, and salt until the mixture reaches 220°F on an instant-read thermometer, about 3 minutes.

1 cup (140 grams) heavy whipping cream

1½ cups (256 grams) bittersweet chocolate, chopped or chips

4 large egg yolks

¼ cup (52 grams) sugar

¼ cup (60 grams) water

2 tablespoons (40 grams) light corn syrup

2 teaspoons (10 grams) vanilla extract

½ teaspoon salt

½ teaspoon powdered gelatin

Immediately remove the pot from the heat, reduce the speed of the mixer to low, and slowly pour the sugar mixture over the egg yolks, with the mixer running, taking care not to pour the hot mixture onto the moving whisk. Add the powdered gelatin and mix until dissolved, about 1 minute. Raise the mixer speed to high and whip until light, fluffy, tripled in volume, and cooled to room temperature, about 6 minutes.

4 Remove the bowl of whipped egg yolks from the mixer, add the melted chocolate, and quickly fold until smooth. Gently fold the whipped cream into the mousse. Cover the mousse with plastic wrap and refrigerate until ready to use, or up to 4 hours.

Note Making chocolate mousse can be a bit tricky. The key is to combine the components when they are at similar temperatures to ensure they blend well. That means don't let the melted chocolate get too hot, and don't let the whipped cream get too cold. If you find that the melted chocolate in your mousse sets up and creates little chips of chocolate when you add the whipped cream, don't fret. This is because the chocolate was a bit too hot, the cream was very cold, or you folded the two together a little too slowly. When this happens, I just call it "chocolate chip mousse" and enjoy it anyway, because the mousse tastes just as delicious!

MEXICAN CHOCOLATE MOUSSE

Add 2 teaspoons (6 grams) ground cinnamon and ½ teaspoon cayenne pepper after the melted chocolate in Step 4.

Lavender–White Chocolate Gâteaux Saint-Honoré

> ⤙○ **MAKES 9 INDIVIDUAL GÂTEAUX** ○⤚

1 Preheat the oven to 375°F. Line a baking sheet with parchment paper.

2 On a lightly floured surface, roll the sheet of puff pastry dough to ⅛ inch thick. Using a 3½-inch round cookie cutter, cut 9 circles from the dough and then place them on the baking sheet. Prick several small holes over the entire surface of the dough circles with a fork, to prevent the dough from rising too much. Transfer the dough to the freezer to harden, about 10 minutes.

3 Remove the dough from the freezer and cover with a sheet of parchment paper and another flat baking sheet, to prevent the puff pastry from rising too much as it bakes. Bake the pastry for about 30 minutes. Carefully remove the top baking sheet and top layer of parchment paper and continue to bake for

Bread flour, for rolling

1 sheet (about 8 ounces) frozen puff pastry dough, thawed

36 Small Cream Puff Shells (page 34)

White Chocolate Mousse (page 137)

White Glaze (page 40), tinted lavender

Purple sanding sugar, for decorating (optional)

Lavender Whipped Cream (page 138)

Blackberries, for decorating

about 5 more minutes, until crisp and deep golden brown. Let the puff pastry cool on the baking sheet.

4 **To assemble the gâteaux:** Place a round piping tip (such as Ateco #802) on the tip of your index finger, or use the tip of a paring knife, and pierce a ¼-inch hole in the bottom of each cream puff shell.

5 Fill a pastry bag fitted with the same round piping tip with the mousse. Piping into the hole in each cream puff, gently fill with mousse, taking care not to overfill. Set aside at room temperature until ready to use.

6 Dip the top of each of the filled cream puffs into the glaze. Sprinkle with purple sugar, if desired, and set aside until the glaze has fully set and hardened, about 20 minutes. Set aside 9 of the cream puffs.

7 Dip the bottoms of the remaining 27 cream puffs into the glaze and then arrange them on the puff pastry in rings of 3, using the glaze to secure them to the puff pastry. Let stand at room temperature until the glaze hardens, about 20 minutes.

8 Fill a pastry bag fitted with a star piping tip (such as Ateco #826) with the whipped cream and pipe 3 stripes of whipped cream between the cream puffs. Pipe a small rosette of cream on top of each gâteau, then place one of the reserved cream puffs on top. Decorate with the blackberries. Serve immediately, or refrigerate for up to 1 day.

WHITE CHOCOLATE MOUSSE

1   In the bowl of a stand mixer fitted with the whisk attachment, whip the cream until soft peaks form. Transfer to another bowl and set aside at room temperature until ready to use.

2   In a heatproof bowl set over a pot of simmering water, melt the white chocolate. Remove from the heat and let stand at room temperature until ready to use.

3   In the clean bowl of the stand mixer, fitted with the whisk attachment, whip the egg yolks on medium speed. Meanwhile, in a small pot, cook the sugar, water, corn syrup, and salt until the mixture reaches 220°F on an instant-read thermometer. Immediately remove the pot from the heat and slowly pour over the egg yolks, with the mixer running, taking care not to pour the hot mixture onto the moving whisk. Add the gelatin and mix until combined. Raise the mixer speed to high and whip until light, fluffy, and cooled to room temperature.

4   Remove the bowl of whipped egg yolks and sugar from the mixer, add the melted chocolate, and quickly fold until smooth. Fold one-quarter of the whipped cream into the

¾ cup (180 grams) heavy whipping cream

1¼ cups (213 grams) white chocolate, chopped or chips

3 large egg yolks

3 tablespoons (39 grams) sugar

2 tablespoons (30 grams) water

1 tablespoon (20 grams) light corn syrup

¼ teaspoon salt

1 teaspoon powdered gelatin

mousse until combined. Add the remaining whipped cream and gently fold until smooth. Use immediately, or refrigerate until ready to use, up to 4 hours.

LAVENDER WHIPPED CREAM

1 In a small saucepan, bring the cream and lavender flowers to a simmer. Remove from the heat and let stand at room temperature to steep for 10 minutes. Strain the mixture through a fine-mesh sieve and refrigerate until cold, about 1 hour.

2 By hand or using a stand mixer fitted with the whisk attachment, whip the lavender-infused cream and confectioners' sugar until stiff peaks form. Set aside in the refrigerator until ready to use, up to 2 hours. If the cream softens while sitting in the refrigerator, re-whip until stiff peaks form before using.

2 cups (480 grams) heavy whipping cream

2 teaspoons (2 grams) dried lavender flowers

¼ cup (30 grams) confectioners' sugar, sifted

Red Velvet Éclairs

1 Place a round piping tip (such as Ateco #802) on the tip of your index finger, or use the tip of a paring knife, and pierce three ¼-inch holes in the bottom of each éclair shell.

2 Fill a pastry bag fitted with the same round piping tip with the whipped cream cheese. Piping into the holes in each éclair, gently fill with the cream cheese.

3 Dip the top one-third of each éclair into the glaze, allowing the excess to drip away from the éclair before inverting. Using a vegetable peeler, shave the bars of white chocolate over the tops of the éclairs. Set aside until the glaze has fully set and hardened, about 20 minutes. As you are dipping the éclairs, adjust the thickness of the glaze as needed (see page 25). Serve immediately, or refrigerate for up to 8 hours.

10 to 12 Large Éclair Shells (page 33)

Whipped Cream Cheese (page 97)

White Glaze (page 40), tinted red

2 (4-ounce) bars (226 grams) white chocolate

Turtle Éclairs

1 Place a round piping tip (such as Ateco #802) on the tip of your index finger, or use the tip of a paring knife, and pierce three ¼-inch holes in the bottom of each éclair shell.

2 Fill a pastry bag fitted with the same round piping tip with the mousse. Piping into the holes in each éclair, gently fill with mousse.

3 Dip the top one-third of each éclair into the glaze, allowing the excess to drip away from the éclair before inverting. Garnish with a generous coating of the chopped pecans. Set aside until the glaze has fully set and hardened, about 20 minutes. As you are dipping the éclairs, adjust the thickness of the glaze as needed (see page 25). Serve immediately, or refrigerate for up to 8 hours.

10 to 12 Large Éclair Shells (page 33)

Caramel Mousse (page 142)

Chocolate Glaze (page 39)

1 cup (120 grams) roasted and salted pecans, chopped

Note My caramel mousse is a bit of a faux caramel mousse, in that it's just a mix of homemade caramel sauce and mascarpone cheese. Don't tell.

Clockwise from top left: Red Velvet Éclairs (page 139), Turtle Éclairs, and Black Forest Éclairs (page 143) ▶

CARAMEL MOUSSE

1 In a small saucepan, bring the sugar, corn syrup, water, and salt to a boil. Cook until the mixture reaches 350°F on an instant-read thermometer. Immediately remove from the heat, slowly add ½ cup of the cream, and whisk until smooth. Transfer the caramel mixture to a heatproof bowl and refrigerate until cold, 1 to 2 hours.

2 Transfer the caramel mixture to the bowl of a stand mixer fitted with the whisk attachment. Add the remaining ½ cup cream and the mascarpone and whip until the mixture thickens and has a consistency similar to softly whipped cream. Refrigerate until ready to use, up to 4 hours.

Note Be careful of steam and bubbling that may occur when you add the cream to the hot caramel.

½ cup (100 grams) sugar

1 tablespoon (20 grams) light corn syrup

1 tablespoon water

½ teaspoon salt

1 cup (240 grams) heavy whipping cream

1½ cups (338 grams) mascarpone cheese

Black Forest Éclairs

1 Using a serrated knife, trim the top one-third of each éclair shell lengthwise and discard the tops.

2 Fill a pastry bag fitted with a round piping tip (such as Ateco #804) with the whipped cream. Fill a second pastry bag fitted with a round piping tip (such as Ateco #806) with the chocolate mousse.

3 Pipe the mousse onto each éclair until filled just to the top of the trimmed shell. Pipe dots of whipped cream and the remaining mousse, irregularly alternating between the two, to cover the entire surface of each éclair.

4 Place 3 or 4 of the brandied cherries on top of the filling, leaving some of the filling exposed. Garnish each éclair with pinches of cacao nibs and silver leaf, if desired. Serve immediately, or refrigerate for up to 8 hours.

10 to 12 Large Cocoa Éclair Shells (page 33)

2 cups (½ recipe) Whipped Cream (page 41)

Bittersweet Chocolate Mousse (page 132)

30 to 48 (about 60 grams) store-bought brandied cherries

Cacao nibs, for decorating (optional)

Silver leaf, for decorating (optional)

Note *Feel free to substitute chopped chocolate chips for the cacao nibs if you don't want to purchase an extra ingredient for this recipe.*

Tiramisu

1 Place eight 4-ounce ramekins on a baking sheet. Using a serrated knife, slice the cream puff shells in half lengthwise and press each half flat with your hands. Transfer the tiramisu filling to a pastry bag without a piping tip.

2 Pipe about one-third of the filling into an even layer over the bases of each ramekin, filling each ramekin about one-third full. Submerge one half of a flattened cream puff in the tiramisu soak and let it absorb the liquid until just soft. Place the soaked cream puff on top of the filling. Repeat the layering with another one-third of the filling, place another soaked cream puff half on top, and then divide the remaining filling evenly among the ramekins to fill. Using an offset metal spatula, spread the top of the filling until perfectly smooth. Cover with plastic wrap pressed directly on the top of the filling and refrigerate for 4 hours to overnight to set. Dust generously with cocoa powder just before serving.

8 Large Cocoa Cream Puff Shells (page 35)

Tiramisu Filling (page 146)

Tiramisu Soak (page 146)

Cocoa powder, for dusting

Note *Use caution when consuming raw eggs due to the slight risk of food-borne illness such as salmonella. To reduce this risk, use grade A or AA eggs that are fresh, have been properly refrigerated, and have their shells intact. Organic, free-range eggs are best.*

Tiramisu and Chocolate Chip Cannoli Éclairs (page 147) ▶

TIRAMISU FILLING

MAKES ABOUT 5 CUPS

1 In the bowl of a stand mixer fitted with the whisk attachment, whip the cream until stiff peaks form. Transfer to another bowl and refrigerate until ready to use.

2 In the clean bowl of the stand mixer, fitted with the whisk attachment, whip the eggs and sugar on high speed until light, fluffy, and tripled in volume, about 8 minutes. Add the mascarpone, amaretto, Kahlúa, and vanilla and whip until thickened and the texture is similar to softened buttercream. Remove the bowl from the mixer and gently fold in the whipped cream until evenly incorporated. Set aside in the refrigerator until ready to use, or up to 1 day.

1 cup (240 grams) heavy whipping cream

2 large eggs

¼ cup plus 1 tablespoon (63 grams) sugar

1¼ cups (280 grams) mascarpone cheese, softened

2 tablespoons (30 grams) amaretto

2 tablespoons (30 grams) Kahlúa

2 teaspoons (10 grams) vanilla extract

TIRAMISU SOAK

MAKES ABOUT 1¼ CUPS

Whisk all the ingredients together in a large bowl until the espresso powder has dissolved.

¾ cup (180 grams) water

¼ cup (60 grams) Kahlúa

¼ cup (60 grams) amaretto

3 tablespoons (12 grams) instant espresso powder

1 tablespoon (15 grams) vanilla extract

Chocolate Chip Cannoli Éclairs

1 Spread the chocolate on a plate and reserve for decorating.

2 Using a serrated knife, cut about ¼ inch off the ends of each éclair shell on a diagonal. Using a chopstick or your finger, press the excess dough in the center of the éclairs to create hollow tubes. Fill a pastry bag fitted with a round piping tip (such as Ateco #805) with the cannoli filling. Pipe the filling into one end of a shell to the center, then into the other end. Repeat with the remaining shells and filling. Dip both ends of each éclair in the chopped chocolate on the plate. Serve immediately, or refrigerate for up to 4 hours.

½ cup (85 grams) finely chopped bittersweet chocolate

16 to 18 Small Cocoa Éclair Shells (page 31)

Chocolate Chip Cannoli Filling (page 148)

CHOCOLATE CHIP CANNOLI FILLING

MAKES ABOUT 2 CUPS

In the bowl of a food processor, puree the ricotta, sugar, lemon zest, cinnamon, and salt until smooth, scraping down the sides of the bowl a few times as it blends. Transfer the mixture to a large bowl, add the chopped chocolate, and fold until smooth. Refrigerate until ready to use, up to 2 days.

2 cups (450 grams) whole-milk ricotta cheese

¼ cup plus 2 tablespoons (76 grams) sugar

Finely grated zest of ¼ lemon

½ teaspoon ground cinnamon

¼ teaspoon salt

½ cup (85 grams) finely chopped bittersweet chocolate

Mississippi Mud Puffs

1 Process the chocolate wafer cookies in a food processor until finely ground. (Alternatively, place the cookies in a resealable plastic bag and pound with a mallet or small pan until finely ground.) Transfer the cookie crumbs to a bowl and set aside.

2 Place a round piping tip (such as Ateco #802) on the tip of your index finger, or use the tip of a paring knife, and pierce a ¼-inch hole in the bottom of each of the cream puff shells.

3 Fill a pastry bag fitted with the same round piping tip with the pastry cream. Piping into the hole in each cream puff, gently fill with pastry cream.

4 Using a fork, dip each cream puff into the melted butter, allowing the excess to drip away. Drop the puffs in the ground chocolate wafer cookies and roll to coat. Transfer to the refrigerator to set, about 10 minutes. Serve immediately, or refrigerate for up to 8 hours.

1 (4½-ounce) package (about 125 grams) chocolate wafer cookies

30 to 36 Small Cocoa Cream Puff Shells (page 34)

Chocolate Pastry Cream (page 38)

1½ sticks (170 grams) unsalted butter, melted and slightly cooled

Note *If you can't find chocolate wafer cookies, you can grind crème-filled chocolate cookies for the crumb coating. (You can also scrape off and eat all the crème filling first, if you're a little piggy like me.)*

Nutella Cream Puffs

MAKES 14 TO 16 CREAM PUFFS

1   Fill a pastry bag fitted with a round piping tip (such as Ateco #802) with the Nutella-mascarpone filling. Using a serrated knife, slice the cream puff shells in half lengthwise, arranging the tops and bottoms side by side.

2   Pipe a large dollop of the filling over the bases of the cream puffs, filling each puff about 1 inch high. Set the tops over the filling. Drizzle with the glaze and generously sprinkle the tops with the chopped hazelnuts. Serve immediately, or refrigerate for up to 1 day.

Nutella-Mascarpone Filling (recipe follows)

14 to 16 Large Cocoa Cream Puff Shells (page 34)

Chocolate Glaze (page 39)

½ cup (70 grams) roasted hazelnuts, finely chopped

Note This filling is far more than a cream puff filling. I use it for a cake or crepe filling, or a cupcake frosting, or I just smear it on toasted bread with a drizzle of olive oil for an afternoon snack.

NUTELLA-MASCARPONE FILLING

MAKES ABOUT 3 CUPS

In a large bowl, fold the Nutella and mascarpone together until smooth. Cover and refrigerate until ready to use, or up to 3 days. If needed, stir the filling to soften before using.

2 cups (600 grams) Nutella

1 cup (225 grams) mascarpone cheese

◀ *Clockwise from top left: Nutella Cream Puffs, Mississippi Mud Puffs (page 149), and Persian-Spiced Chocolate Cream Puffs (page 152)*

Persian-Spiced Chocolate Cream Puffs

1 Place a round piping tip (such as Ateco #802) on the tip of your index finger, or use the tip of a paring knife, and pierce a ¼-inch hole in the bottom of each cream puff shell.

2 Fill a pastry bag fitted with the same round piping tip with the pastry cream. Piping into the hole in each cream puff, gently fill with pastry cream.

3 Dip the top of each cream puff into the glaze, allowing the excess to drip away from the cream puff before inverting. Very generously sprinkle the tops of the puffs with the spice topping to completely coat the glaze. Set the puffs aside at room temperature until the glaze has fully set and hardened, about 20 minutes. As you are dipping the cream puffs, adjust the thickness of the glaze as needed (see page 25). Serve immediately, or store in the refrigerator for up to 1 day.

14 to 16 Large Cocoa Cream Puff Shells (page 35)

Chocolate Pastry Cream (page 38)

Chocolate Glaze (page 39)

Persian Spice Topping (page 153)

PERSIAN SPICE TOPPING

1 In a dry skillet, toast the sesame, coriander, and cumin seeds over medium heat until fragrant, light golden brown, and the seeds just begin to pop. Pour onto a plate and let cool to room temperature.

2 Transfer the toasted spices to the bowl of a food processor. Add the pistachios, hazelnuts, coconut, salt, and pepper, and pulse until finely ground. Store in an airtight container at room temperature until ready to use, up to 1 month.

Note *This recipe makes about twice as much of the topping as you will need for the cream puffs. Use the extra to sprinkle over a bowl of hummus, as a crust for lamb or chicken, or as a topping for a chocolate sundae.*

¼ cup (36 grams) sesame seeds

2 tablespoons (12 grams) coriander seeds

2 tablespoons (18 grams) cumin seeds

¼ cup (35 grams) roasted pistachios

¼ cup (35 grams) roasted hazelnuts

¼ cup (20 grams) unsweetened shredded coconut

½ teaspoon salt

¼ teaspoon ground black pepper

S'mores Éclairs

Using a serrated knife, cut the éclair shells in half lengthwise. Place the éclairs on an unlined baking sheet. Scatter the marshmallows on the top half of each éclair. Scatter the chopped chocolates on the bottom halves. With a handheld kitchen torch, gently melt the chocolate (alternatively, microwave the éclair halves with the chocolate until melted). Then, with the handheld kitchen torch, gently toast the marshmallows to a light golden brown (alternatively, set the baking sheet in the broiler to gently toast the marshmallows to a light golden brown, 1 to 2 minutes). Press the tops and bottoms together and serve immediately.

16 to 18 Small Éclair Shells (page 31)

1 (10-ounce) bag (about 280 grams) miniature marshmallows

1 (4-ounce) bar (113 grams) bittersweet chocolate, chopped

1 (4-ounce) bar (113 grams) milk chocolate, chopped

1 (4-ounce) bar (113 grams) white chocolate, chopped

Note If you prefer more highbrow s'mores, make the Bittersweet Chocolate Mousse on page 132 and the Italian Meringue on page 113 for the fillings and skip the chopped chocolate and miniature marshmallows.

Chocolate and Churros

1 In a medium saucepan, bring the water, milk, sugar, butter, and salt to a rolling boil. Turn off the heat and add the flour all at once, while continuing to stir. Turn the heat to medium-low and cook the dough, stirring constantly, until it forms a ball and leaves a skin on the base of the pot, 3 to 4 minutes.

2 Transfer the dough to a large bowl. Add the whole eggs, one at a time, stirring vigorously to combine between each addition. Scrape down the sides of the bowl with a rubber spatula as needed between each addition. Add the egg whites and mix the dough until the eggs are fully combined and the mixture is smooth. Fill a pastry bag fitted with a star piping tip (such as Ateco #824) with the dough and refrigerate until ready to use.

3 Line two baking sheets with parchment paper and lightly coat them with nonstick cooking spray. Pipe the dough in lines, 2 to 2½ inches in length. Place the baking sheets with the dough

½ cup (120 grams) water

½ cup (120 grams) whole milk

1 tablespoon (13 grams) sugar

6 tablespoons (84 grams) unsalted butter

¼ teaspoon salt

1 cup (128 grams) unbleached all-purpose flour

3 large eggs

2 large egg whites

Nonstick cooking spray

Canola oil, for frying

Spiced Sugar (page 159)

Hot Chocolate Dipping Sauce (page 159)

strips in the freezer until fully hardened, about 30 minutes, or until ready to fry.

4 **To fry the churros:** Heat 2 inches of oil in a heavy pot to 375°F on an instant-read thermometer. Place a cooling rack over a baking sheet.

5 Carefully remove the strips of dough from the parchment paper and drop into the oil. Continue to add the churros to the oil, taking care to leave about 1 inch of space between each piece. Fry the churros until deep golden brown, 3 to 4 minutes on each side. Using a slotted spoon, carefully remove the churros and set on the rack. Sprinkle generously with the spiced sugar while still warm and serve with the dipping sauce. Churros are best served warm, but they can be made 1 day ahead and stored at room temperature until ready to serve.

Note Save the original container the oil was purchased in and, once cooled to room temperature, pour it back into the container to store for reuse or disposal. You can reuse oil for frying two or three times before disposing of it. Simply strain the oil before reusing.

SPICED SUGAR

Combine the sugar, cinnamon, and salt together in a small bowl. Set aside until ready to use.

½ cup (100 grams) sugar

1 teaspoon ground cinnamon

¼ teaspoon salt

HOT CHOCOLATE DIPPING SAUCE

1 Stir the sugar, cornstarch, and salt together in a small bowl.

2 Bring the milk to a boil in a medium pot. Remove from the heat, add the chocolate, and whisk until smooth. Add the sugar mixture and cook over medium-low heat, while whisking constantly, until the sauce thickens, 10 to 12 minutes. Remove from the heat and whisk until smooth. Divide the dipping sauce among small cups and serve warm with the churros.

½ cup (100 grams) sugar

2 tablespoons (16 grams) cornstarch

¼ teaspoon salt

4 cups (960 grams) whole milk

1⅓ cups (227 grams) bittersweet chocolate, chopped or chips

Chocolate and Sea Salt Seashells

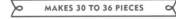
1 Preheat the oven to 350°F. Line a baking sheet with parchment paper.

2 Fill a pastry bag fitted with a star piping tip (such as Ateco #866) with the pâte à choux dough. Pipe the dough into shells about 1 inch wide and 1½ inches long by holding the tip at a 45-degree angle and squeezing the dough onto the baking sheet. While continuing to apply pressure, gently lift the tip slightly up and then gradually relax the pressure as you lower the tip and pull the bag toward you until the tip reaches the surface of the baking sheet. Stop the pressure and pull the bag away to make the dough come to a point. Leave about ½ inch of space between each shell.

3 Lightly brush each shell with the beaten egg and sprinkle with the sea salt. Bake for 40 to 45 minutes, until puffed, dry on the surface, and cooked through in the center. Serve immediately, while warm.

Cocoa Pâte à Choux Dough (page 29)

1 large egg, lightly beaten

1 tablespoon (10 grams) flaky sea salt, such as Maldon brand

Note Don't skimp on the sea salt. It may seem like a lot, but once baked, these pastries are deliciously salty and sweet.

Frozen

Strawberry-Buttermilk Sherbet Parfaits

MAKES 8 SERVINGS

1 Toss the strawberries with the brown sugar and salt, and let stand at room temperature to macerate until the juices release from the fruit and the sugar dissolves, about 10 minutes.

2 Remove the sherbet from the freezer to soften. By hand, tear the cream puff shells into small pieces.

3 By hand or using a stand mixer fitted with the whisk attachment, whip the cream until soft peaks form. Refrigerate until ready to use.

4 Just before serving, assemble the parfaits: In 8 small serving glasses or dessert bowls, layer a couple teaspoons of the cream puff shell pieces, a few heaping spoonfuls of sherbet, some macerated strawberries, and a dollop of whipped cream. Repeat the layers until the glasses are full. Serve immediately.

1 pound (454 grams) ripe strawberries, hulled and quartered

3 tablespoons (42 grams) light brown sugar

¼ teaspoon salt

Strawberry-Buttermilk Sherbet (page 166), or 2 pints store-bought

16 Small Cream Puff Shells (page 34)

1½ cups (360 grams) heavy whipping cream

Note *Because the pâte à choux in this recipe is torn into small pieces, it doesn't matter how expertly the shells are piped, making this a great beginner recipe for practicing your piping skills.*

STRAWBERRY-BUTTERMILK SHERBET

MAKES ABOUT 1 QUART

1 Combine all the ingredients in a blender and puree until liquefied. Strain the mixture through a fine-mesh sieve and refrigerate until cold, about 2 hours.

2 Freeze the mixture in an ice cream machine according to the manufacturer's instructions until the sherbet has a smooth, creamy texture. Store in the freezer for 4 hours before serving, or up to 4 weeks.

⅔ **pound (300 grams) ripe strawberries, hulled and quartered**

2 cups (490 grams) buttermilk

1¼ cups (250 grams) sugar

¼ cup (80 grams) light corn syrup

Juice of ½ lemon

¼ teaspoon salt

Note If you have any leftover empty cream puff or éclair shells from recipes you've already made, don't throw them away. Pop them in a resealable plastic bag and freeze them until you are ready to make parfaits.

Peachy Parfaits

1 Preheat the oven to 450°F. Line a baking sheet with aluminum foil and lightly coat with nonstick cooking spray.

2 In a bowl, toss the peaches, honey, salt, and cinnamon together. Spread the fruit into a single layer on the baking sheet and roast until the fruit just begins to brown on the edges, about 25 minutes. Let cool to room temperature.

3 Remove the sorbet from the freezer to soften. Tear the cream puff shells into small pieces.

4 By hand or using a stand mixer fitted with the whisk attachment, whip the cream until soft peaks form. Refrigerate until ready to use.

5 Just before serving, assemble the parfaits: In 8 small serving glasses or dessert bowls, layer a couple teaspoons of cream puff shell pieces, a few heaping spoonfuls of sorbet, some peach slices, and a dollop of whipped cream. Repeat until the glasses are full. Serve immediately.

Nonstick cooking spray

8 ripe peaches, pitted and sliced

2 tablespoons (40 grams) honey

¼ teaspoon salt

¼ teaspoon ground cinnamon

Peach Sorbet (page 168), or 2 pints store-bought

16 Small Cream Puff Shells (page 34)

1½ cups (360 grams) heavy whipping cream

Note The best way to roast fruit is with very high heat. As it cooks, you will smell their sugars burning and they may possibly create smoke—this is okay and will make for delicious flavor.

PEACH SORBET

MAKES ABOUT 1 QUART

1 Pit and cut the peaches in half, keeping the skins on.

2 In a large saucepot, bring all of the ingredients to a full boil. Reduce the heat to medium and simmer until the fruit is soft and just beginning to break down, about 15 minutes. Remove from the heat, transfer the mixture to a heatproof bowl, and place over a large bowl of ice water. Stir occasionally until the peach mixture is cooled to room temperature.

3 Transfer the mixture to a blender and puree until completely smooth. Strain the mixture through a fine-mesh sieve into a container and refrigerate the sorbet base overnight.

4 Freeze the sorbet base in an ice cream machine according to the manufacturer's instructions until the sorbet has a smooth, creamy texture. Store in the freezer for 4 hours before serving, or up to 4 weeks.

10 very ripe peaches

1¼ cups (300 grams) sweet white wine, such as Sauternes

1¼ cups (250 grams) sugar

½ cup (120 grams) water

¼ teaspoon salt

Seeds from 1 vanilla bean

Mocha Profiteroles

1 Remove the ice cream from the freezer to soften. With a serrated knife, slice the cream puff shells in half horizontally, setting the tops next to their corresponding bottoms.

2 Using an ice cream scoop dipped into warm water, place a scoop of ice cream on the bottom of each cream puff, then set the top of each cream puff on the ice cream. Place the assembled profiteroles on a baking sheet and transfer to the freezer to set, about 20 minutes.

3 **To serve:** Set two profiteroles on a serving dish, drizzle with the chocolate sauce, and garnish with a pinch of chocolate-covered espresso beans, if desired.

2 pints coffee ice cream (see Note, page 59, or store-bought)

14 or 16 Large Cocoa Cream Puff Shells (page 35)

Chocolate Sauce (page 59)

Chocolate-covered espresso beans, finely chopped, for decorating (optional)

Note *Profiteroles can be assembled and frozen up to 3 days in advance of serving. Lightly cover them with plastic wrap or store them in an airtight container, then drizzle them with sauce and garnish with the espresso beans just before serving.*

▲ *Pumpkin Pie Profiteroles (page 179), Salty Caramel-Almond Profiteroles (page 176), Butterscotch Bombs, and Mocha Profiteroles (page 169)*

Butterscotch Bombs

1 Remove the ice cream from the freezer to soften. With a serrated knife, slice the cream puff shells in half horizontally, setting the tops next to their corresponding bottoms.

2 Using a small ice cream scoop dipped into warm water, place a scoop of ice cream on the bottom of each cream puff, then set the top of each cream puff on the ice cream. Place the assembled profiteroles on a baking sheet and transfer to the freezer to set, about 20 minutes.

3 **To serve:** Set two profiteroles on a serving dish, drizzle with the butterscotch sauce, and garnish with a pinch of the butterscotch candies, if desired. Serve immediately.

Butterscotch Ice Cream (page 172), or 2 pints store-bought

14 or 16 Large Cream Puff Shells (page 35)

Butterscotch Sauce (page 173)

Butterscotch candies, finely chopped, for decoration (optional)

Note Profiteroles can be assembled and frozen up to 3 days in advance of serving. Lightly cover them with plastic wrap or store them in an airtight container, then drizzle them with sauce and garnish with the butterscotch candies just before serving.

BUTTERSCOTCH ICE CREAM

1 In a medium bowl, whisk the cornstarch, xanthan gum, and salt until well combined. Add the milk and cream and whisk until well combined.

2 In a medium pot, cook the brown sugar and butter over medium-high heat until the mixture is bubbly, 3 to 4 minutes. Add the milk mixture, reduce the heat to low, and bring to a simmer. Cook, whisking occasionally, until thickened, 8 to 10 minutes. Strain the mixture through a fine-mesh sieve into a large metal bowl. Add the Scotch and vanilla. Place the bowl of ice cream base over another bowl of ice water and stir until the base is cooled to room temperature. Refrigerate until cold, about 2 hours.

3 Freeze the ice cream base in an ice cream machine according to the manufacturer's instructions until the ice cream has a smooth, soft-serve texture. Store in the freezer for 4 hours to set before serving, or up to 4 weeks.

1 tablespoon (8 grams) cornstarch

½ teaspoon xanthan gum

¼ teaspoon salt

2 cups (480 grams) whole milk

1½ cups (360 grams) heavy whipping cream

¾ cup (168 grams) firmly packed dark brown sugar

2 tablespoons (28 grams) unsalted butter

2 tablespoons (30 grams) Scotch or bourbon

1 tablespoon (15 grams) vanilla extract

Note If you choose to use store-bought ice cream, butterscotch might not be the easiest flavor to find. Either caramel or butter pecan would be a fine substitute.

BUTTERSCOTCH SAUCE

In a small saucepan, melt the butter. Add the cream, brown sugar, and salt and bring to a boil. Reduce the heat and let simmer until thickened, stirring occasionally, about 10 minutes. Remove from the heat, add the Scotch and vanilla, and let cool to room temperature. Cover and refrigerate until ready to use, up to 1 week. Serve warm or chilled.

4 tablespoons (56 grams) unsalted butter

½ cup (120 grams) heavy whipping cream

½ cup (112 grams) firmly packed dark brown sugar

¾ teaspoon salt

2 tablespoons (30 grams) Scotch or bourbon

1 tablespoon (15 grams) vanilla extract

Vanilla Malt Profiteroles

1 Remove the ice cream from the freezer to soften. Using a serrated knife, slice the cream puff shells in half horizontally, setting the tops next to their corresponding bottoms.

2 Using a small ice cream scoop dipped into warm water, place a scoop of ice cream on the bottom of each cream puff, then set the top of each cream puff on the ice cream. Place the assembled profiteroles on a baking sheet and transfer to the freezer to set, about 20 minutes.

3 **To serve:** Set two profiteroles on a serving dish, drizzle with the white chocolate sauce, and garnish with a pinch of chopped malted milk balls, if desired. Serve immediately.

Vanilla Bean Ice Cream (page 59), or 2 pints store-bought

14 or 16 Large Cream Puff Shells (page 35)

Malted White Chocolate Sauce (page 175)

Malted milk balls, finely chopped, for topping (optional)

Note If you're more of a chocolate malt fan, fill the profiteroles with chocolate ice cream.

Note Profiteroles can be assembled and frozen up to 3 days in advance of serving. Lightly cover them with plastic wrap or store them in an airtight container, then drizzle them with sauce and garnish with the malted milk balls just before serving.

MALTED WHITE CHOCOLATE SAUCE

1   Place the white chocolate in a medium bowl.

2   In a small saucepan, bring the cream, barley malt syrup, malted milk powder, and salt to a boil. Remove from the heat and pour over the white chocolate. Let the mixture stand for 2 minutes to soften the chocolate, then whisk until smooth. Serve warm.

Note Barley malt syrup is a dark brown and very sticky sweetener made from sprouted barley. It looks a lot like molasses, but has a distinctly "malty" flavor. Jars of it can be found alongside the honey and maple syrup in most natural or gourmet food stores.

⅔ cup (113 grams) white chocolate, chopped or chips

¼ cup plus 2 tablespoons (90 grams) heavy whipping cream

3 tablespoons (45 grams) barley malt syrup

2 tablespoons (18 grams) malted milk powder

¼ teaspoon salt

Salty Caramel-Almond Profiteroles

1 Remove the ice cream from the freezer to soften. Using a serrated knife, slice the cream puff shells in half horizontally, setting the tops next to their corresponding bottoms.

2 Using a small ice cream scoop dipped into warm water, place a scoop of ice cream on the bottom of each cream puff, then set the top of each cream puff on the ice cream. Place the assembled profiteroles on a baking sheet and transfer to the freezer to set, about 20 minutes.

3 To serve: Set two profiteroles on a serving dish, drizzle with the caramel sauce, and garnish with a pinch of chopped almonds. Serve immediately.

Salty Caramel-Almond Ice Cream (page 177), or 2 pints store-bought

14 or 16 Large Cream Puff Shells (page 35)

Caramel Sauce (page 178)

Roasted almonds, finely chopped, for garnish

Note Profiteroles can be assembled and frozen up to 3 days in advance of serving. Lightly cover them with plastic wrap or store them in an airtight container, then drizzle them with sauce and garnish with the almonds just before serving.

SALTY CARAMEL-ALMOND ICE CREAM

MAKES ABOUT 1 QUART

1 In a small bowl, whisk the cornstarch, salt, and xanthan gum until well combined.

2 In a medium pot, bring the sugar, water, and corn syrup to a boil. Cook until the mixture reaches 380°F on an instant-read thermometer. The caramel will be very dark in color and begin to smoke slightly. Immediately remove from the heat and very slowly add the milk and cream. If the caramel seizes, continue to whisk until it dissolves. Slowly sprinkle the cornstarch mixture over the surface of the caramel mixture, while whisking constantly, until fully dissolved. Return to the stove, bring to a simmer, and cook, whisking occasionally, for 8 to 10 minutes, until thickened. Strain the mixture through a fine-mesh sieve into a large metal bowl. Place the bowl of ice cream base over another bowl of ice water and stir until the base is cooled to room temperature. Refrigerate until cold, about 2 hours.

3 Freeze the ice cream base in an ice cream machine according to the manufacturer's instructions until the ice cream has a smooth, soft-serve texture. Quickly add the chopped

1 tablespoon (8 grams) cornstarch

¾ teaspoon salt

½ teaspoon xanthan gum

¾ cup (150 grams) sugar

2 tablespoons (30 grams) water

1 tablespoon (20 grams) light corn syrup

2 cups (480 grams) whole milk

1½ cups (360 grams) heavy whipping cream

¾ cup (105 grams) roasted almonds, roughly chopped

almonds and fold until evenly dispersed in the ice cream. Store in the freezer for 4 hours to set before serving, or up to 4 weeks.

Note If you would prefer to use store-bought ice cream, it may not be easy to find salted caramel and almond ice cream, but you can certainly find caramel ice cream easily enough in your local grocery store. To make your store-bought caramel ice cream perfect for this recipe, let it soften just a bit and then fold chopped almonds and sea salt into the ice cream. Pack it back in the ice cream containers and freeze until it hardens again.

CARAMEL SAUCE

MAKES ABOUT 1 CUP

In a small saucepan, bring the sugar, water, corn syrup, and salt to a boil. Cook until the mixture reaches 380°F on an instant-read thermometer. The caramel will be very dark in color and begin to smoke slightly. Immediately remove from the heat, and very slowly add the cream, whisking until smooth. If the caramel seizes, continue to whisk until it dissolves. Transfer the mixture to a heatproof bowl and let stand at room temperature until ready to use, up to 2 hours.

½ cup (100 grams) sugar

2 tablespoons (30 grams) water

1 tablespoon (20 grams) light corn syrup

¼ teaspoon salt

½ cup (120 grams) heavy whipping cream

Note Be careful of steam and bubbling that may occur when you add the cream to the hot caramel.

Pumpkin Pie Profiteroles

1 Remove the ice cream from the freezer to soften. With a serrated knife, slice the cream puff shells in half horizontally, setting the tops next to their corresponding bottoms.

2 Using an ice cream scoop dipped into warm water, place a scoop of ice cream on the bottom of each cream puff, then set the top of each cream puff on the ice cream. Place the assembled profiteroles on a baking sheet and transfer to the freezer to set, about 20 minutes.

3 **To serve:** Set two profiteroles on a serving dish and dust with confectioners' sugar. Serve immediately.

Pumpkin Pie Ice Cream (page 180), or 2 pints store-bought

14 or 16 Large Cream Puff Shells (page 35)

Confectioners' sugar, for dusting

Note Profiteroles can be assembled and frozen up to 3 days in advance of serving. Lightly cover them with plastic wrap or store them in an airtight container, then dust with confectioners' sugar just before serving.

PUMPKIN PIE ICE CREAM

1 In a medium bowl, whisk the cornstarch, xanthan gum, cinnamon, salt, ginger, and nutmeg until well combined. Add the milk and cream and whisk until well combined.

2 In a medium pot, bring the maple syrup to a simmer and cook until reduced by half, about 10 minutes. Add the milk-spice mixture and bring to a simmer. Cook, whisking occasionally, for 8 to 10 minutes, until thickened. Remove from the heat and add the pumpkin puree. Strain the mixture through a fine-mesh sieve into a large metal bowl. Place the bowl of ice cream base over another bowl of ice water and stir until the base is cooled to room temperature. Refrigerate until cold, about 2 hours.

3 Freeze the ice cream base in an ice cream machine according to the manufacturer's instructions until the ice cream has a smooth, soft-serve texture. Store in the freezer for 4 hours to set before serving, or up to 4 weeks.

1 tablespoon (8 grams) cornstarch

½ teaspoon xanthan gum

½ teaspoon ground cinnamon

¼ teaspoon salt

¼ teaspoon ground ginger

¼ teaspoon ground nutmeg

2 cups (480 grams) whole milk

1½ cups (360 grams) heavy whipping cream

1 cup (315 grams) maple syrup, preferably Grade A Dark Robust

1 cup (250 grams) pumpkin puree

Note You can use homemade roasted pumpkin puree or canned pumpkin puree. Be sure to purchase plain pumpkin puree and not canned pumpkin pie filling, which is already seasoned.

Pistachio-Raspberry Swirl Éclairs

1 Using a serrated knife, cut the éclair shells in half lengthwise and set the tops and bottoms next to each other on a baking sheet. Dip the top of each éclair into the glaze, allowing the excess to drip away from the éclair before inverting. Sprinkle the tops generously with pistachios and freeze-dried raspberries, if desired. Place the tops back on the baking sheet and set aside in the freezer until the glaze has fully set and hardened, about 5 minutes. As you are dipping the éclairs, adjust the thickness of the glaze as needed (see page 25). Meanwhile, remove the ice cream from the freezer to soften.

2 Remove the éclair shells from the freezer. Using a small ice cream scoop dipped into warm water, place a row of ice cream scoops on the bottom of each éclair shell. Set the top of each éclair on the ice cream. Transfer to the freezer to set, about 20 minutes, or until ready to serve.

10 to 12 Large Éclair Shells (page 33)

White Glaze (page 40), tinted pink

Pistachios, finely chopped, for decorating (optional)

Freeze-dried raspberries, finely chopped, for decorating (optional)

Pistachio-Raspberry Swirl Ice Cream (page 183), or 2 pints store-bought pistachio ice cream (see Note, page 183)

Note If you can't find freeze-dried raspberries, you can garnish the éclairs with homemade dried raspberries. Just scatter fresh raspberries on a baking sheet and bake at 100°F for up to 10 hours, until completely dry and brittle. Let cool and then store in an airtight container until ready to use.

PISTACHIO-RASPBERRY SWIRL ICE CREAM

MAKES ABOUT 1 QUART

1 In a medium pot, whisk the sugar, cornstarch, xanthan gum, and salt until well combined. Add the milk and cream and bring to a simmer. Cook, whisking occasionally, until thickened, 8 to 10 minutes. Remove from the heat, add the pistachio paste, and whisk until smooth. Strain the mixture through a fine-mesh sieve into a large metal bowl. Place the bowl of ice cream base over another bowl of ice water and stir until the base is cooled to room temperature. Refrigerate until cold, about 2 hours.

2 Freeze the ice cream base in an ice cream machine according to the manufacturer's instructions until the ice cream has a smooth, soft-serve texture. Gently fold the raspberry jam into the ice cream to swirl. Store in the freezer for 4 hours to set before serving, or up to 4 weeks.

½ cup (100 grams) sugar

1 tablespoon (8 grams) cornstarch

½ teaspoon xanthan gum

¼ teaspoon salt

3 cups (720 grams) whole milk

1 cup (240 grams) heavy whipping cream

½ cup (150 grams) pistachio paste or pistachio butter

¾ cup (about 225 grams) seedless raspberry jam

Note For a really quick version of this ice cream, let 2 pints of store-bought pistachio ice cream soften a bit and then fold the raspberry jam into the ice cream to swirl. Pack it back in the ice cream containers and freeze until it hardens again.

Orange Creamsicle Éclairs

1 Remove the ice cream and sherbet from the freezer to soften. Using a serrated knife, cut off and discard the top one-third of the éclair shells.

2 Using a small ice cream scoop dipped into warm water, place a row of ice cream scoops on the bottom of each éclair shell, alternating between scoops of vanilla ice cream and orange sherbet. Garnish with kumquat slices, if desired. Place the assembled éclairs on a baking sheet and transfer to the freezer to set, about 20 minutes or until ready to serve.

Vanilla Bean Ice Cream (page 59), or 2 pints store-bought

2 pints orange sherbet

10 to 12 Large Éclair Shells (page 33)

Kumquats, thinly sliced, for decorating (optional)

Orange Creamsicle Éclairs and Key Lime Pie Éclairs (page 186) ▶

Key Lime Pie Éclairs

1 Remove the ice cream from the freezer to soften. Using a serrated knife, cut the éclair shells in half lengthwise and discard the tops. Break the graham crackers into small pieces.

2 Using a small ice cream scoop dipped into warm water, place a row of ice cream scoops on the bottom of each éclair shell. Place the assembled éclairs on a baking sheet and transfer to the freezer to set, about 20 minutes.

3 By hand or using a stand mixer fitted with the whisk attachment, whip the cream until stiff peaks form. Transfer the whipped cream to a pastry bag fitted with a star piping tip (such as Ateco #824). Set aside in the refrigerator until ready to use, up to 2 hours.

4 **To serve:** Pipe a small rosette on top of each scoop of ice cream. Garnish each rosette with a small piece of graham cracker and serve immediately.

Key Lime Ice Cream (page 187), or 2 pints store-bought

10 to 12 Large Éclair Shells (page 33)

2 full-size graham crackers

1 cup (240 grams) heavy whipping cream

Note *Don't feel like making Key lime ice cream? That's OK! Just fold freshly grated lime zest into softened vanilla ice cream to taste. Pack the ice cream back in the containers and freeze until it hardens again.*

KEY LIME ICE CREAM

1 In a medium pot, whisk the sugar, cornstarch, xanthan gum, and salt until well combined. Add the cream, milk, half of the lime zest, and the lime juice and bring to a simmer. Cook, whisking occasionally, until thickened, 8 to 10 minutes. Strain the mixture through a fine-mesh sieve into a large metal bowl. Add the remaining lime zest. Place the bowl of ice cream base over another bowl of ice water and stir until the base is cooled to room temperature. Refrigerate until cold, about 2 hours.

2 Freeze the ice cream base in an ice cream machine according to the manufacturer's instructions until the ice cream has a smooth, soft-serve texture. Store in the freezer for 4 hours to set before serving, or up to 4 weeks.

¾ cup (150 grams) sugar

1 tablespoon (8 grams) cornstarch

½ teaspoon xanthan gum

¼ teaspoon salt

1½ cups (360 grams) heavy whipping cream

1 cup (240 grams) whole milk

Finely grated zest of 4 limes

1 cup (240 grams) Key lime juice

Mint Chocolate Chip Ice Cream Cake

◁ꞁ MAKES ONE 8-INCH ROUND CAKE ꞁ▷

1 Preheat the oven to 350°F. Line four baking sheets with parchment paper. (If you don't have four baking sheets, the remaining dough can stand at room temperature while you bake in batches.)

2 Fill a pastry bag fitted with a round piping tip (such as Ateco #806) with the pâte à choux dough and pipe 4 disks, one on each baking sheet, about 8 inches in diameter and ⅜ inch thick. Lightly moisten a fingertip with cold water and gently smooth any peaks or points created when piping. Bake 2 disks for 35 to 40 minutes, until cooked through in the center. Let cool on the baking sheets to room temperature, and bake the remaining disks. Set the base of an 8-inch springform pan on top of each disk to use as a guide and trim the disks to a perfect 8-inch circle.

3 recipes Cocoa Pâte à Choux Dough (page 29)

2 quarts (2 recipes) Mint Chocolate Chip Ice Cream (page 192), or 2 quarts store-bought

Italian Meringue (page 193)

Note *Be sure to cut the ice cream cake with a serrated knife, dipped into warm water, just before serving. The cake will slice much more easily.*

3   Remove the ice cream from the freezer to soften. Re-assemble the springform pan and have ready a second 8-inch springform pan.

4   Press one of the pâte à choux rings into the bottom of a springform pan. Top with heaping spoonfuls of ice cream to make a 1-inch-thick layer, and smooth with an offset spatula to remove any air pockets. Top with a second disk of pâte à choux and press it firmly onto the ice cream. Top with more ice cream to fill to the top of the springform pan, and smooth with an offset spatula. Repeat with the remaining 2 disks and the remaining ice cream in the second springform pan to make a second ice cream cake. Cover the top of the cakes with plastic wrap and freeze for at least 6 hours or up to overnight to firmly set.

5   Remove the cakes from the freezer, unwrap, and discard the plastic wrap. Use a handheld kitchen torch to lightly warm the sides of the pans, or let the cakes stand at room temperature until the ice cream just begins to soften, and then remove the outer ring of each springform pan. Remove the springform bottoms from the bottom of the cakes and stack the cakes on top of one another. Place the cake on a large serving platter and return the cake to the freezer to set, about 45 minutes.

6 Mound the meringue onto the top of the cake and, using a large offset spatula, ice the top and sides of the cake with a thick, even layer of meringue. Apply a bit of pressure to the tip of the spatula as you are frosting to create a swirled texture. Serve immediately, or freeze until ready to serve, up to 1 week.

Note This recipe works best using two 8-inch springform pans. However, if you only have one, you can still make it: Either spread the ice cream a little thinner in order to fit all four layers in one pan; or make the cake in two batches, freezing the first half entirely and transferring it to the serving platter before assembling and freezing the second half using the same pan.

MINT CHOCOLATE CHIP ICE CREAM

MAKES ABOUT 1 QUART

1 In a medium pot, whisk the sugar, cornstarch, xanthan gum, and salt until well combined. Add the milk, cream, and mint leaves and bring to a simmer. Cook, whisking occasionally, until thickened, 8 to 10 minutes. Strain the mixture through a fine-mesh sieve into a large metal bowl. Place the bowl of ice cream base over another bowl of ice water and stir until the base is cooled to room temperature. Add food coloring if desired, one drop at a time, and stir until the ice cream base reaches the desired color. Refrigerate until cold, about 2 hours.

2 Freeze the ice cream base in an ice cream machine according to the manufacturer's instructions until the ice cream has a smooth, soft-serve texture. Quickly add the chopped chocolate and fold until evenly dispersed in the ice cream. Store in the freezer for 4 hours to set before serving, or up to 4 weeks.

½ cup (100 grams) sugar

1 tablespoon (8 grams) cornstarch

½ teaspoon xanthan gum

¼ teaspoon salt

2 cups (480 grams) whole milk

1½ cups (360 grams) heavy whipping cream

1 cup (30 grams) fresh mint leaves, stems removed

Green gel paste food coloring (optional)

½ cup (85 grams) chopped semisweet chocolate

ITALIAN MERINGUE

MAKES ABOUT 4 CUPS

1 In the bowl of a stand mixer fitted with the whisk attachment, whip the egg whites on low speed.

2 Meanwhile, combine the sugar, water, honey, and salt in a small saucepan and cook over medium heat until the mixture reaches 238°F on an instant-read thermometer, about 12 minutes.

3 Immediately remove from the heat, raise the mixer speed to medium-high, and very slowly pour the hot sugar mixture over the egg whites, taking care not to pour the hot mixture onto the moving whisk.

4 Raise the mixer speed to high and whip until tripled in volume, thick, glossy, and cooled to room temperature, about 10 minutes. Refrigerate until ready to use, up to 4 hours (or freeze in an airtight container for up to 1 week).

4 large egg whites

1⅓ cups (267 grams) sugar

½ cup (120 grams) water

1 tablespoon (20 grams) honey

¼ teaspoon salt

Banana Split Éclairs

1 Remove the ice cream from the freezer to soften. Using a serrated knife, cut the éclair shells in half lengthwise, placing the tops next to their corresponding bottoms.

2 Using a small ice cream scoop dipped into warm water, place a row of ice cream scoops on the bottom of each éclair shell, then set the top of each éclair on the ice cream. Place the assembled éclairs on a baking sheet and transfer to the freezer to set, about 20 minutes.

3 By hand or using a stand mixer fitted with the whisk attachment, whip the cream until stiff peaks form. Set aside in the refrigerator until ready to use.

4 **To serve:** Transfer the whipped cream to a pastry bag fitted with a star piping tip (such as Ateco #824). Drizzle each éclair with the chocolate sauce, pipe a small rosette of whipped cream on top, and place a cherry in the center of the rosette. Garnish with sprinkles, if desired, and serve immediately.

Banana Ice Cream (page 196), or 2 pints store-bought

10 to 12 Large Éclair Shells (page 33)

1 cup (240 grams) heavy whipping cream

Chocolate Sauce (page 59)

10 to 12 maraschino cherries

Multicolored sprinkles, for decorating (optional)

BANANA ICE CREAM

1 In a medium pot, whisk the sugar, cornstarch, xanthan gum, and salt until well combined. Add the milk and cream and bring to a simmer. Cook, whisking occasionally, until thickened, 8 to 10 minutes. Strain the mixture through a fine-mesh sieve. Transfer the mixture to a blender. Add the bananas and puree until smooth. Pour the ice cream base into a large metal bowl. Place the bowl of ice cream base over another bowl of ice water and stir until the base is cooled to room temperature. Refrigerate until cold, about 2 hours.

2 Freeze the ice cream base in an ice cream machine according to the manufacturer's instructions until the ice cream has a smooth, soft-serve texture. Store in the freezer for 4 hours to set before serving, or up to 4 weeks.

½ cup (100 grams) sugar

1 tablespoon (8 grams) cornstarch

½ teaspoon xanthan gum

¼ teaspoon salt

2 cups (480 grams) whole milk

1½ cups (360 grams) heavy whipping cream

4 (about 400 grams) very ripe bananas, chopped

Note If you really want to go bananas, try tossing the bananas with a little sugar and then roasting them before using them in the ice cream. It will give the ice cream an even richer banana flavor.

Cookies and Cream
Ice Cream Sandwiches

◇ MAKES 8 TO 10 ICE CREAM SANDWICHES ◇

1   Preheat a pizzelle iron according to the manufacturer's instructions.

2   Lightly coat the iron with nonstick cooking spray and spoon about 1½ tablespoons of the pâte à choux dough onto the center of the pizzelle press. Cook the pizzelles until the steam from the dough stops escaping from the sides of the press, about 1½ minutes. Repeat with the remainder of the dough. Set aside 16 to 20 of the nicest-looking pizzelles. In the bowl of a food processor, grind the remaining 4 to 8 pizzelles into crumbs and reserve for making the Cookies and Cream Ice Cream (page 199).

3   Remove the ice cream from freezer to soften.

4   Using an ice cream scoop dipped into warm water, place a scoop of ice cream on half of the pizzelles. Set a second pizzelle on top of the ice cream and gently press to sandwich. Using a

Nonstick cooking spray

Cocoa Pâte à Choux Dough (page 29)

Cookies and Cream Ice Cream (page 199), or 2 pints store-bought

Note Don't forget to save the extra pizzelles to be used in the Cookies and Cream Ice Cream recipe.

small offset spatula, smooth the sides of the ice cream, if needed. Place the assembled ice cream sandwiches on a baking sheet and transfer to the freezer to set before serving, about 30 minutes.

COOKIES AND CREAM ICE CREAM

MAKES ABOUT 1 QUART

1   In a medium pot, whisk the sugar, cornstarch, xanthan gum, and salt until well combined. Add the milk and cream and bring to a simmer. Cook, whisking occasionally, until thickened, 8 to 10 minutes. Strain the mixture through a fine-mesh sieve into a large metal bowl. Place the bowl of ice cream base over another bowl of ice water and stir until the base is cooled to room temperature. Refrigerate until cold, about 2 hours.

2   Freeze the ice cream base in an ice cream machine according to the manufacturer's instructions until the ice cream has a smooth, soft-serve texture. Gently fold the pizzelle crumbs into the ice cream. Store in the freezer for 4 hours to set before serving, or up to 4 weeks.

½ cup (100 grams) sugar

1 tablespoon (8 grams) cornstarch

½ teaspoon xanthan gum

¼ teaspoon salt

2 cups (480 grams) whole milk

1½ cups (360 grams) heavy whipping cream

Cocoa Pâte à Choux pizzelle crumbs, reserved from page 197 (from 4 to 8 cookies)

◀ *Cookies and Cream Ice Cream Sandwiches and Honey-Cinnamon Ice Cream Sandwiches (page 200)*

Honey-Cinnamon Ice Cream Sandwiches

1 Remove the ice cream from the freezer to soften.

2 Using an ice cream scoop dipped into warm water, place a scoop of ice cream on half of the pizzelles. Set a second pizzelle on top of the ice cream and gently press to sandwich. Using a small offset spatula, smooth the sides of the ice cream, if needed. Place the assembled ice cream sandwiches on a baking sheet and transfer to the freezer to set before serving, about 30 minutes.

Honey-Cinnamon Ice Cream (page 201), or 2 pints store-bought

16 to 20 Pâte à Choux Pizzelles (page 280)

Note Save any extra pizzelles for snacking, or use them as crackers for a cheese board as suggested in the Note on page 280.

HONEY-CINNAMON ICE CREAM

MAKES ABOUT 1 QUART

1 In a medium pot, whisk the cornstarch, xanthan gum, cinnamon, and salt until well combined. Add the milk, cream, and honey and bring to a simmer. Cook, whisking occasionally, until thickened, 8 to 10 minutes. Strain the mixture through a fine-mesh sieve into a large metal bowl. Place the bowl of ice cream base over another bowl of ice water and stir until the base is cooled to room temperature. Refrigerate until cold, about 2 hours.

2 Freeze the ice cream base in an ice cream machine according to the manufacturer's instructions until the ice cream has a smooth, soft-serve texture. Store in the freezer for 4 hours to set before serving, or up to 4 weeks.

1 tablespoon (8 grams) cornstarch

½ teaspoon xanthan gum

½ teaspoon ground cinnamon

¼ teaspoon salt

2 cups (480 grams) whole milk

1½ cups (360 grams) heavy whipping cream

¾ cup (240 grams) honey

Chocolate-Coconut Gâteaux Saint-Honoré

1 Preheat the oven to 375°F. Line a baking sheet with parchment paper.

2 On a lightly floured surface, roll the sheet of puff pastry dough to ⅛ inch thick. Using a 3½-inch round cookie cutter, cut 9 circles from the dough, and place them on the baking sheet. Prick several small holes over the entire surface of the dough circles with a fork, to prevent the dough from rising too much. Transfer the dough to the freezer to harden, about 15 minutes.

3 Remove the dough from the freezer and cover with a sheet of parchment paper and another flat baking sheet, to prevent the puff pastry from rising too much as it bakes. Bake the pastry for about 30 minutes. Remove the top baking sheet and top layer of parchment paper and continue to bake the puff pastry for about

Bread flour, for rolling

1 sheet (about 8 ounces) frozen puff pastry dough, thawed

Coconut Sherbet (page 205), or 2 pints store-bought

36 Small Cream Puff Shells (page 34)

Chocolate Glaze (page 39)

Coconut Whipped Cream (page 205)

Note *Making all of the components from scratch for this recipe is an all-day affair, enough to make even the most seasoned baker go, well, coconuts. I suggest dividing the labor over a few days, or purchasing a good-quality coconut sherbet or sorbet to save a bit of time.*

5 more minutes, until crisp and deep golden brown. Let cool on the baking sheet to room temperature.

4 Remove the sherbet from the freezer to soften.

5 **To assemble the gâteaux:** Slice the cream puff shells in half horizontally, setting the tops next to their corresponding bottoms.

6 Using an ice cream scoop dipped into warm water, place a scoop of sherbet on the bottom of each cream puff, then set the top of each cream puff on the sherbet. Place the assembled puffs on a baking sheet and transfer to the freezer to set, about 20 minutes. Remove from the freezer and drizzle each puff with the chocolate glaze. Return to the freezer until ready to use.

7 Working with one gâteau at a time, generously spread about a tablespoon of glaze on the surface of a disk of puff pastry. Arrange three sherbet-filled puffs in a circle on the puff pastry, using the glaze to secure them. (You will still have 9 cream puffs remaining.) Place the assembled gâteaux on a baking sheet and transfer to the freezer to set, about 20 minutes, or until ready to serve, up to 4 days.

8 Just before serving, fill a pastry bag fitted with a star piping tip (such as Ateco #826) with the whipped cream. Remove the assembled gâteaux from the freezer and pipe 3 stripes of whipped cream between the cream puffs. Pipe a small rosette of cream on top of each gâteau, then place one of the remaining cream puffs on top of each rosette. Serve immediately.

COCONUT SHERBET

MAKES ABOUT 1 QUART

1 Combine all the ingredients in a large pot and bring to a boil. Reduce the heat to a simmer and cook, stirring occasionally, for about 10 minutes. Remove from the heat and let cool until warm enough to handle. Strain the mixture through a fine-mesh sieve into a large metal bowl. Place the bowl of warm sherbet base over another bowl of ice water and stir until the base is cooled to room temperature. Refrigerate until cold, about 2 hours.

2 Freeze the sherbet base in an ice cream machine according to the manufacturer's instructions until it has a smooth, creamy texture. Store in the freezer overnight to set before serving, or up to 4 weeks.

2¼ cups (540 grams) whole milk

1½ cups (375 grams) canned coconut milk

1½ cups (120 grams) unsweetened shredded coconut

1½ cups (300 grams) sugar

¾ cup (200 grams) canned cream of coconut, such as Coco Lopez

1 tablespoon (15 grams) vanilla extract

¼ teaspoon salt

COCONUT WHIPPED CREAM

MAKES ABOUT 3 CUPS

By hand or using a stand mixer fitted with the whisk attachment, whip the cream, confectioners' sugar, and coconut extract until stiff peaks form. Cover and refrigerate until ready to use, up to 2 hours. If the cream softens while sitting in the refrigerator, re-whip until stiff peaks form before using.

1½ cups (360 grams) heavy whipping cream

3 tablespoons (21 grams) confectioners' sugar, sifted

1 teaspoon coconut extract

Holiday

Valentine's Day Rose Water Hearts

1 Preheat the oven to 350°F. Line two baking sheets with parchment paper.

2 Fill a pastry bag fitted with a star piping tip (such as Ateco #827) with the pâte à choux dough and pipe hearts 3 to 4 inches wide, leaving about 1 inch of space between each heart. Lightly moisten a fingertip with cold water and gently smooth any peaks or points created when piping. Bake for 40 to 45 minutes, until deep golden brown and cooked through in the center. Let cool on the baking sheet to room temperature.

Pâte à Choux Dough (page 28)

Rose Water Glaze (page 211)

Pink dragées, for decorating (optional)

3   Dip the top half of each heart into the glaze, allowing the excess to drip away from the heart before inverting. Sprinkle with pink dragées, if desired. As you are dipping the hearts, adjust the thickness of the glaze as needed (see page 25). Set aside to allow the glaze to set, about 20 minutes, and then serve immediately.

ROSE WATER GLAZE

Sift the confectioners' sugar into a large bowl. Add the water, corn syrup, rose water, and salt and whisk by hand until smooth. The glaze should have a thick consistency that still allows for dipping. To make a thicker glaze, slowly add sifted confectioners' sugar until the glaze reaches the desired consistency. To make a thinner glaze, add water, 1 teaspoon at a time. Add food coloring, one drop at a time, stirring until evenly combined, until the glaze reaches the desired color. Cover the bowl with plastic wrap and set aside at room temperature until ready to use, up to 1 day.

1½ cups (180 grams) confectioners' sugar, plus more for adjusting glaze

¼ cup (60 grams) water, plus more for adjusting glaze

2 tablespoons (40 grams) light corn syrup

1 teaspoon rose water

¼ teaspoon salt

Pink gel paste food coloring (optional)

Mardi Gras King Cakes

MAKES 8 TO 10 KING CAKES

1 Using a serrated knife, slice the Paris-Brest shells in half horizontally, setting the tops next to their corresponding bottoms. Gently spread a thick coating of glaze on each of the tops and immediately sprinkle with colored sugars to decorate, if desired. Set aside to allow the glaze to set, about 20 minutes.

2 Gently spread a heaping tablespoon of the strawberry jam on the bottom of each Paris-Brest shell. Fill a pastry bag fitted with a star piping tip (such as Ateco #827) with the whipped cream cheese and pipe it on top of the strawberry jam, dividing evenly among the Paris-Brest shells. Gently place the Paris-Brest tops on the whipped cream cheese. Serve immediately, or refrigerate for up to 8 hours.

8 to 10 Paris-Brest Shells (page 36)

White Glaze (page 40)

Purple, green, and gold sanding sugar or sprinkles, for decorating (optional)

¾ cup (about 315 grams) strawberry jam

Whipped Cream Cheese (page 97)

Note To color your own sugars, rub a few drops of food coloring and granulated sugar together until you have the desired color. Don't forget to wear rubber gloves!

Easter Eggs

1 Preheat the oven to 350°F. Line a baking sheet with parchment paper.

2 Fill a pastry bag fitted with a round piping tip (such as Ateco #806) with the pâte à choux dough. Pipe the dough by holding the tip at a 45-degree angle and squeezing the dough onto the baking sheet while slowly pulling the piping tip back to create an oval shape that is about the size of a large egg, leaving about 1 inch of space between each oval. Bake for 40 to 45 minutes, until deep golden brown and cooked through in the center. Let cool on the baking sheet to room temperature.

3 Place a round piping tip (such as Ateco #802) on the tip of your index finger, or use the tip of a paring knife, and pierce a ¼-inch hole in the bottom of each of the Easter eggs.

4 Fill a pastry bag fitted with the same round piping tip with the pastry cream. Piping into the hole in each Easter egg, gently fill with pastry cream.

Pâte à Choux Dough (page 28)

Vanilla Bean Pastry Cream (page 37)

White Glaze (page 40), tinted as desired

Assorted pastel-colored edible glitters and luster dusts, for decorating

Gold and silver leaf sheets, for decorating

Note When decorating with gold or silver leaf, use a small paintbrush or toothpick to remove the leaves from their book and place them on the glazed eggs.

5 Dip the top two-thirds of each Easter egg into the colored glaze, allowing the excess to drip away from the Easter egg before inverting. Decorate with assorted glitters, luster dusts, and gold or silver leaf. Set aside until the glaze has fully set and hardened, about 20 minutes. Serve the Easter eggs immediately.

Note To create the torn gold and silver leaf effect in the photo (page 214), place a large piece of the leaf on the glaze while it's wet. As the excess wet glaze drips down the sides of the egg, the leaf will tear and take on an abstract look.

Mother's Day Éclairs

1 Place a round piping tip (such as Ateco #802) on the tip of your index finger, or use the tip of a paring knife, and pierce three ¼-inch holes in the bottom of each éclair shell.

2 Fill a pastry bag fitted with the same round piping tip with the pastry cream. Piping into the holes in each éclair, gently fill with pastry cream.

3 Drizzle the tops of the éclairs with the glaze. Decorate with fresh flowers and dragées, if desired. Set aside until the glaze has fully set and hardened, about 20 minutes.

10 to 12 Large Éclair Shells (page 33)

Lemon Pastry Cream (page 219)

Lemon Glaze (page 220)

Fresh edible flowers, such as pansies, for decorating (optional)

Purple dragées, for decorating (optional)

LEMON PASTRY CREAM

MAKES ABOUT 3 CUPS

1 In a large bowl, whisk the egg yolks, egg, and cornstarch together until completely smooth.

2 In a medium pot, bring the milk, sugar, salt, and lemon zest to a boil. Slowly pour the hot milk over the egg yolks while whisking constantly. Return the mixture to the pot and cook over medium-low heat, whisking constantly but slowly, until just thickened and bubbles rise to the surface, about 4 minutes. Increase the speed of whisking to smooth the custard and continue to cook until it has thickened to the consistency of pudding and coats the back of a spoon, about 2 minutes.

3 Immediately remove the pot from the heat, add the butter, and whisk until fully melted and smooth. Strain the mixture through a fine-mesh sieve into a large bowl and cover the pastry cream with a sheet of plastic wrap directly on the surface to prevent a skin from forming. Refrigerate until cold and fully set, about 2 hours, or up to 3 days.

4 large egg yolks

1 large egg

¼ cup plus 3 tablespoons (53 grams) cornstarch

2 cups (480 grams) whole milk

½ cup plus 2 tablespoons (126 grams) sugar

¼ teaspoon salt

Finely grated zest of 2 lemons

5 tablespoons (70 grams) unsalted butter, cut into small pieces

LEMON GLAZE

MAKES ABOUT ¾ CUP

Sift the confectioners' sugar into a large bowl. Add the corn syrup, lemon zest and juice, and salt and whisk by hand until smooth. The glaze should have a thick consistency that still allows for dipping. To make a thicker glaze, slowly add sifted confectioners' sugar until the glaze reaches the desired consistency. To make a thinner glaze, add lemon juice, 1 teaspoon at a time. Add food coloring, one drop at a time, stirring until evenly combined, until the glaze reaches the desired color. Cover the bowl with plastic wrap and set aside at room temperature until ready to use, up to 4 hours.

1½ cups (180 grams) confectioners' sugar, plus more for adjusting glaze

2 tablespoons (40 grams) light corn syrup

Finely grated zest of 2 lemons

2 tablespoons (28 grams) freshly squeezed lemon juice, plus more for adjusting glaze

¼ teaspoon salt

Yellow gel paste food coloring (optional)

Fourth of July Sparklers

1 Preheat the oven to 350°F. Line two baking sheets with parchment paper.

2 Fill a pastry bag fitted with a star piping tip (such as Ateco #862) with the pâte à choux dough and pipe straight lines, 8 inches long and ¼ inch wide, onto the baking sheets, leaving about ½ inch of space between each. (If desired, use a ruler to draw 8-inch wide columns on the parchment paper to serve as a tracing guide when piping. Be sure to place the parchment paper marked side down on the baking sheets before piping the dough.) Lightly moisten a fingertip with cold water and gently smooth any peaks or points created when piping. Bake for 25 to 30 minutes, until deep golden brown. Let cool on the baking sheets to room temperature.

3 Gently melt the white chocolate in a heatproof bowl set over a pan of simmering water. Remove from the heat.

Pâte à Choux Dough (page 28)

1½ cups (255 grams) white chocolate, chopped or chips

Red, white, blue, and silver nonpareils or sprinkles

4 Dip one end of each pâte à choux stick into the melted white chocolate, allowing the excess to drip from the stick, to create a thin coating. Immediately decorate the dipped ends of the sticks with nonpareils. Set the sparklers on a baking sheet and refrigerate until the chocolate fully hardens, about 20 minutes. Serve immediately, or refrigerate for up to 8 hours.

Halloween Spider Webs

1 Fill a pastry bag fitted with a coupler and a small round piping tip (such as Ateco #1) with the royal icing. On a sheet of waxed paper, carefully pipe about 24 spider webs, about 2 inches in diameter. (The decorations are very delicate and often break when removed from the waxed paper, so it is necessary to make extras.) Let stand at room temperature to harden for 4 hours or up to overnight.

2 Place a round piping tip (such as Ateco #802) on the tip of your index finger, or use a paring knife, and pierce a ¼-inch hole in the bottom of each cream puff shell.

3 Fill a pastry bag fitted with the same round piping tip with the pastry cream. Piping into the hole in each cream puff, gently fill with pastry cream.

Royal Icing (page 41)

14 to 16 Large Cream Puff Shells (page 35)

Vanilla Bean Pastry Cream (page 37)

Chocolate Glaze (page 39)

Note You can print an image of a spider web outline, from the Internet or another source, and place it under the waxed paper to use as a stencil when piping your decorations.

4   Very carefully remove the spider webs from the waxed paper by loosening with a small metal offset spatula and peeling the waxed paper away. Dip the top of each cream puff into the glaze, allowing the excess to drip away from the cream puff before inverting. As you are dipping the cream puffs, adjust the thickness of the glaze as needed (see page 25). Carefully place one spider web on the top of each cream puff and set aside until the glaze has fully set and hardened, about 20 minutes. Serve immediately.

Day of the Dead Éclairs

1   Fill a pastry bag fitted with a coupler and a small round piping tip (such as Ateco #1) with royal icing. On a sheet of waxed paper, carefully pipe the outline of 18 skulls, about 1 inch in diameter. On another sheet of waxed paper, pipe the outlines of several small flowers and scroll decorations. Transfer the colored icing(s) to a paper cornet (see Note, page 228) and, using the cornet, fill in the outlines of the skulls, flowers, and scrolls in your desired colors, ensuring all the lines of icing connect to create a solid decoration. (The decorations are very delicate and often break when removed from the waxed paper, so it is necessary to make extras.) Let stand at room temperature to harden for 4 hours or up to overnight.

2   Place a round piping tip (such as Ateco #802) on the tip of your index finger, or use the tip of a paring knife, and pierce three ¼-inch holes in the bottom of each éclair shell.

Royal Icing (page 41), tinted as desired (optional)

10 to 12 Large Cocoa Éclair Shells (page 33)

Mexican Chocolate Mousse (page 133)

Chocolate Glaze (page 39)

Note If the idea of making royal icing skulls and decorations makes you want to drop dead, skip them! The spicy chocolate mousse filling and chocolate glaze are good enough to honor the dead.

3 Fill a pastry bag fitted with the same round piping tip with the chocolate mousse. Piping into the holes in each éclair, gently fill with mousse.

4 Dip the top one-third of each éclair into the glaze, allowing the excess to drip away from the éclair before inverting. Carefully remove the decorations from the waxed paper and place on top of the éclairs. Set aside until the glaze has fully set and hardened, about 20 minutes. As you are dipping the éclairs, adjust the thickness of the glaze as needed (see page 25). Serve immediately, or refrigerate for up to 8 hours.

Note A paper cornet (pictured on page 218) is a small piping bag made from parchment paper that is used for making fine decorations. To use one, roll a triangle of parchment paper into a cone shape (search for tutorials online if you need help). Fill the cone no more than two-thirds full with icing. Fold the top corners of the cone inward, then fold the top of the cone down at least twice to close the cone. Using sharp scissors, trim the very tip of the cone to create a small hole to pipe.

Thanksgiving Turkeys

1 Fill a pastry bag fitted with a coupler and a very small round piping tip (such as Ateco #1) with the royal icing. On a sheet of waxed paper, carefully pipe each turkey tail in the shape of a fan. Start with the smallest feathers and work outward to create three rows of feathers, ensuring all of the lines of piped icing connect. Repeat to make 24 tails. (The decorations are very delicate and often break when removed from the waxed paper, so it is necessary to make extras.) Let stand at room temperature to harden for 4 hours or up to overnight.

2 On another sheet of waxed paper, pipe the outline of 24 turkey heads, about 1½ inches tall and ½ inch wide, with the royal icing, taking care to include the shape of the beak and wattle. Let stand at room temperature to harden, about 30 minutes. Carefully fill in the outline of each turkey head with royal icing, piping a small dot for the eye and a second layer of icing to accentuate the beak and wattle. Let stand at room temperature to harden for

Royal Icing (page 41)

Red, orange, and yellow petal dusts

14 to 16 Large Cream Puff Shells (page 35)

Vanilla Bean Pastry Cream (page 37)

Note *Make extra royal icing feathers and heads, as they tend to break easily. If they break, don't fret. You can use a little more royal icing to glue them back together. Let them dry until they have fully hardened again before decorating and attaching to the cream puff shells.*

4 hours or up to overnight. Reserve the remaining icing in the pastry bag, inserting a toothpick into the piping tip to prevent the icing from drying out by sealing the bag from air.

3 Keeping the piped decorations on the waxed paper and using small paintbrushes, paint the tails with the red, orange, and yellow petal dusts to create an ombré pattern. Paint the heads lightly with the red petal dust, and paint the wattles with a second layer of red petal dust. Paint the beaks with the yellow petal dust.

4 Place a round piping tip (such as Ateco #802) on the tip of your index finger, or use the tip of a paring knife, and pierce a ¼-inch hole in the bottom of each cream puff shell.

5 Fill a pastry bag fitted with the same round piping tip with the pastry cream. Piping into the hole in each cream puff, gently fill with pastry cream.

6 Very carefully remove the turkey heads and tails from the waxed paper by loosening with a small metal offset spatula and peeling the waxed paper away.

7 Using a paring knife, cut a small and narrow slit in the top of each cream puff to match the width of each turkey head. Carefully insert a turkey head into each slit. Secure the heads with a thin line of piped icing, if needed, and hold in place until the icing hardens, about 5 minutes.

8 Working with one tail at a time, pipe a thin line of the reserved icing along the bottom edge of the tail. Gently press the tail against the cream puff and pipe additional icing to secure the tail to the cream puff so that is it well adhered. Hold the tail in place by propping it against something stable (such as a rolling pin set on a kitchen towel or a stack of cookbooks) until the icing hardens, about 20 minutes. Repeat to attach the remaining tails. Serve the cream puffs immediately.

Note *Oftentimes, a ridge emerges on the top of large cream puff shells as they bake. This ridge is a great place to affix the turkey's tail feathers, as it hides the additional royal icing needed to secure them in place.*

Hanukkah Sufganiyot (Jelly Doughnuts)

MAKES 20 TO 24 DOUGHNUTS

1 In a medium saucepan, bring the water, milk, butter, granulated sugar, and ¼ teaspoon of the salt to a rolling boil. Remove from the heat and add the flour all at once, while continuing to stir. Turn the heat to medium-low and cook the dough, while stirring constantly, until it forms a ball and leaves a skin on the base of the pot, 3 to 4 minutes.

2 Transfer the dough to a large bowl. Add the whole eggs, one at a time, stirring vigorously to combine between each addition. Scrape down the sides of the bowl with a rubber spatula as needed between each addition. Add the egg whites and mix the dough until the eggs are fully combined and the mixture is smooth.

3 To fry the sufganiyot: Heat 2 inches of oil in a heavy pot to 375°F on an instant-read thermometer. Stir the superfine sugar, cinnamon, cardamom, and the remaining ½

½ cup (120 grams) water

½ cup (120 grams) whole milk

6 tablespoons (85 grams) unsalted butter

1 tablespoon (13 grams) granulated sugar

¾ teaspoon salt

1 cup (128 grams) unbleached all-purpose flour

3 large eggs

2 large egg whites

Canola oil, for frying

1 cup (100 grams) superfine sugar

2 teaspoons (6 grams) ground cinnamon

½ teaspoon ground cardamom

2½ cups (about 375 grams) seedless raspberry jam

teaspoon salt together in a large bowl for coating the doughnuts later. Place a rack on a baking sheet and set aside.

4 Using a 1- to 1½-ounce cookie scoop, carefully drop one scoop of dough at a time into the oil. Continue to add more dough to the oil, taking care to leave about 1 inch of space between each piece. Fry the sufganiyot until deep golden brown, 5 to 7 minutes. Using a slotted spoon, carefully remove the sufganiyot from the oil, allowing the excess oil to drain back into the pot. Immediately transfer them to the bowl of superfine sugar and gently toss to completely coat in sugar. Set on the rack to cool until cool enough to handle.

5 Place a round piping tip (such as Ateco #802) on the tip of your index finger, or use the tip of a paring knife, and pierce a ¼-inch hole in the bottom of each doughnut.

6 Fill a pastry bag fitted with the same round piping tip with the raspberry jam. Piping into the hole in each doughnut, gently fill with jam. Serve immediately.

Note Professional doughnut makers use a pastry tip called a bismarck to pierce and fill doughnuts with jam or cream in one step. It is a long pastry tip with a pointed end (pictured on page 19) and worth purchasing if you like to make homemade doughnuts often.

Snowflakes

MAKES ABOUT 10 SNOWFLAKES

1 Preheat the oven to 350°F. Line two baking sheets with parchment paper. Draw the outline of 5 snowflakes, 3 to 4 inches in diameter, on each piece of parchment paper. Flip the paper over on the baking sheets, so the side with the writing is facing down.

2 Fill a pastry bag fitted with a very small round piping tip (such as Ateco #6) with the pâte à choux dough and pipe onto the baking sheets, tracing the lines of the snowflakes on the parchment paper. Bake the snowflakes for 16 to 20 minutes, until light golden brown. Let cool on the baking sheets.

3 Have the coconut ready in a shallow bowl. Dip the top of each snowflake into the glaze, allowing the excess to drip away before inverting. Immediately press the snowflake into the coconut to coat the glaze. Set aside at room temperature until the glaze hardens, about 20 minutes. Serve immediately, or store in an airtight container for up to 2 days.

Pâte à Choux Dough (page 28)

1 cup (80 grams) unsweetened shredded coconut, for coating

White Glaze (page 40)

Note If you'd like to make this recipe simpler, you can omit the glaze and coconut and just dust the snowflakes with confectioners' sugar.

Note You can print an image of a snowflake outline, from the Internet or another source, and place it under the parchment paper to use as a stencil for piping the pâte à choux.

Christmas Wreaths

1 Using a serrated knife, slice the Paris-Brest shells in half horizontally, setting the tops next to their corresponding bottoms.

2 Spread a very thick coating of glaze on each of the tops and immediately sprinkle with the peppermint to decorate. Set aside to allow the glaze to set, about 20 minutes. Fill a pastry bag fitted with a star piping tip (such as Ateco #827) with the whipped cream and pipe it in rings, dividing evenly among the Paris-Brest bases. Place the tops on the whipped cream. Serve immediately, or refrigerate for up to 8 hours.

8 to 10 Paris-Brest Shells (page 36)

White Glaze (page 40)

30 peppermint hard candies, finely chopped, for decorating

Peppermint Cream (recipe follows)

PEPPERMINT CREAM

MAKES ABOUT 4 CUPS

By hand or using a stand mixer fitted with the whisk attachment, whip the cream, confectioners' sugar, and peppermint extract until stiff peaks form. Refrigerate until ready to use or up to 2 hours.

2 cups (480 grams) heavy whipping cream

½ cup (60 grams) confectioners' sugar, sifted

½ teaspoon peppermint extract

◀ *Christmas Wreaths and Snowflakes (page 237)*

Gingerbread Éclairs

1 In a food processor, process the gingersnaps into finely ground crumbs, or crush by hand. Spread the crumbs on a large plate and set aside. Place a round piping tip (such as Ateco #802) on the tip of your index finger, or use the tip of a paring knife, and pierce three ¼-inch holes in the bottom of each éclair.

2 Fill a pastry bag fitted with the same round piping tip with the pastry cream. Piping into the holes in each éclair, gently fill with pastry cream.

3 Dip the top one-third of each éclair into the glaze, allowing the excess to drip away from the éclair before inverting. Roll the glazed éclairs in the ground gingersnap crumbs to completely coat the glaze. Set aside until the glaze has fully set and hardened, about 20 minutes. As you are dipping the éclairs, adjust the thickness of the glaze as needed (see page 25). Serve immediately, or refrigerate for up to 8 hours.

15 (about 100 grams) gingersnap cookies

10 to 12 Large Éclair Shells (page 33)

Gingerbread Pastry Cream (page 242)

White Glaze (page 40)

Note *If you want to dress up your gingerbread pastry cream a bit, try adding a bit of orange zest to brighten the flavor. It's an unexpected, but lovely, flavor combination.*

▲ *Gingerbread Éclairs and Eggnog Éclairs (page 243)*

GINGERBREAD PASTRY CREAM

1 In a large bowl, whisk the egg yolks, egg, and cornstarch until completely smooth.

2 In a medium pot, bring the milk, sugar, molasses, ginger, cinnamon, cloves, allspice, salt, and pepper to a boil. Slowly pour the hot milk over the egg yolks while whisking constantly. Return the mixture to the pot and cook over medium-low heat, while whisking constantly but slowly, until just thickened and bubbles rise to the surface, about 4 minutes. Increase the speed of whisking to smooth the custard and continue to cook until it has thickened to the consistency of pudding and coats the back of a spoon, about 2 more minutes.

3 Immediately remove the pot from the heat, add the butter, and whisk until fully melted and smooth. Strain the mixture through a fine-mesh sieve into a large bowl and cover the pastry cream with a sheet of plastic wrap directly on the surface to prevent a skin from forming. Refrigerate until cold and fully set, about 2 hours, or up to 3 days.

4 large egg yolks

1 large egg

¼ cup plus 3 tablespoons (53 grams) cornstarch

2 cups (480 grams) whole milk

½ cup plus 2 tablespoons (126 grams) sugar

¼ cup (90 grams) molasses

2 teaspoons ground ginger

1 teaspoon ground cinnamon

½ teaspoon ground cloves

½ teaspoon ground allspice

¼ teaspoon salt

¼ teaspoon ground black pepper

5 tablespoons (70 grams) unsalted butter, cut into small pieces

Eggnog Éclairs

1 Place a round piping tip (such as Ateco #802) on the tip of your index finger, or use the tip of a paring knife, and pierce three ¼-inch holes in the bottom of each éclair shell.

2 Fill a pastry bag fitted with the same round piping tip with the pastry cream. Piping into the holes in each éclair, gently fill with pastry cream.

3 Dip the top one-third of each éclair into the glaze, allowing the excess to drip away from the éclair before inverting. Sprinkle with freshly grated nutmeg, if desired. Set aside until the glaze has fully set and hardened, about 20 minutes. As you are dipping the éclairs, adjust the thickness of the glaze as needed (see page 25). Serve immediately, or refrigerate for up to 8 hours.

10 to 12 Large Éclair Shells (page 33)

Eggnog Pastry Cream (page 244)

Rum-Nutmeg Glaze (page 245)

Whole nutmeg, for grating (optional)

Note This recipe is truly seasonal, as finding eggnog in the grocery store before November or after December is nearly impossible.

EGGNOG PASTRY CREAM

1 In a large bowl, whisk the egg yolks, egg, and cornstarch until completely smooth.

2 In a medium pot, bring the eggnog, sugar, and salt to a boil. Slowly pour the hot eggnog over the egg yolks while whisking constantly. Return the mixture to the pot and cook over medium-low heat, whisking constantly but slowly, until just thickened and bubbles rise to the surface, about 4 minutes. Increase the speed of whisking to smooth the custard and continue to cook until it has thickened to the consistency of pudding and coats the back of a spoon, about 2 more minutes.

3 Immediately remove the pot from the heat, add the butter and vanilla, and whisk until fully melted and smooth. Strain the mixture through a fine-mesh sieve into a large bowl and cover the pastry cream with a sheet of plastic wrap directly on the surface to prevent a skin from forming. Refrigerate until cold and fully set, about 2 hours, or up to 3 days.

4 large egg yolks

1 large egg

¼ cup plus 3 tablespoons (53 grams) cornstarch

2 cups (530 grams) eggnog

½ cup (100 grams) sugar

¼ teaspoon salt

5 tablespoons (70 grams) unsalted butter, cut into small pieces

1 teaspoon vanilla extract

RUM-NUTMEG GLAZE

Sift the confectioners' sugar and nutmeg into a large bowl. Add the remaining ingredients and whisk by hand until smooth. The glaze should have a thick consistency that still allows for dipping. To make a thicker glaze, slowly add sifted confectioners' sugar until the glaze reaches the desired consistency. To make a thinner glaze, add rum, 1 teaspoon at a time. Cover the bowl with plastic wrap and set aside at room temperature until ready to use, or up to 1 day.

1½ cups (180 grams) confectioners' sugar, plus more for adjusting glaze

1 teaspoon ground nutmeg

2 tablespoons (40 grams) light corn syrup

2 tablespoons (28 grams) rum, plus more for adjusting glaze

¼ teaspoon salt

New Year's Eve Champagne Poppers

⊱ MAKES 30 TO 36 SMALL CREAM PUFFS ⊰

1 Place a round piping tip (such as Ateco #802) on the tip of your index finger, or use the tip of a paring knife, and pierce a ¼-inch hole in the bottom of each cream puff shell.

2 Fill a pastry bag fitted with the same round piping tip with the sabayon. Piping into the hole in each cream puff, gently fill with the sabayon.

3 Dip the top of each cream puff into the glaze, allowing the excess to drip away from the puff before inverting. Decorate with gold decorations and set aside until the glaze has fully set and hardened, about 20 minutes. As you are dipping the cream puffs, adjust the thickness of the glaze as needed (see page 25). Serve immediately, or refrigerate for up to 1 day.

30 to 36 Small Cream Puff Shells (page 34)

Champagne Sabayon (page 248)

Champagne Glaze (page 249)

Assorted gold decorations, such as dragées, edible gold leaf, edible glitter, and sprinkles

CHAMPAGNE SABAYON

1 In a medium saucepan, bring about 2 inches of water to a simmer.

2 Whisk the egg yolks, Champagne, sugar, salt, and gelatin, if using, in a large heatproof bowl that is a few inches wider than the saucepan. Place the bowl over the simmering water and cook, while whisking constantly, until thickened, light in color, and an instant-read thermometer reads 170°F, 8 to 10 minutes. Place the bowl of sabayon over another larger bowl of ice water and stir occasionally until the sabayon reaches room temperature.

3 In the bowl of a stand mixer fitted with the whisk attachment, whip the cream until stiff peaks form. Gently fold the whipped cream into the sabayon, cover the bowl with plastic wrap, and refrigerate until chilled and set, about 2 hours, or up to 1 day.

8 large egg yolks

¾ cup (170 grams) Champagne

¼ cup plus 2 tablespoons (76 grams) sugar

¼ teaspoon salt

¾ teaspoon powdered gelatin (optional)

¾ cup (180 grams) heavy whipping cream

Note *If you prefer not to use gelatin in this recipe, that is fine. The filling will just be a bit softer.*

CHAMPAGNE GLAZE

MAKES ABOUT ¾ CUP

Sift the confectioners' sugar into a large bowl. Add the corn syrup, Champagne, and salt and whisk by hand until smooth. The glaze should have a thick consistency that still allows for dipping. To make a thicker glaze, slowly add sifted confectioners' sugar until the glaze reaches the desired consistency. To make a thinner glaze, add Champagne, 1 teaspoon at a time. Add food coloring, one drop at a time, stirring until evenly combined, until the glaze reaches the desired color. Cover the bowl with plastic wrap and set aside at room temperature until ready to use or up to 1 day.

1½ cups (180 grams) confectioners' sugar, plus more for adjusting glaze

2 tablespoons (40 grams) light corn syrup

2 tablespoons (30 grams) Champagne, plus more for adjusting glaze

¼ teaspoon salt

Beige gel paste food coloring

Savory

Everything "Bagels"

1 Preheat the oven to 350°F. Line two baking sheets with parchment paper.

2 Using a glass or cookie cutter, trace circles about 2¾ inches in diameter on the parchment paper, leaving 2 inches of space between each circle. Flip the parchment so the traced side is facing down. In a small bowl, stir all the seeds and spices together.

3 Fill a pastry bag fitted with a star piping tip (such as Ateco #827) with the pâte à choux dough and pipe rings, following the traced circles. Lightly brush the dough with the beaten egg and generously sprinkle with the seed-spice blend. Bake for 40 to 45 minutes, until deep golden brown and cooked through in the center. Let cool on the baking sheets to room temperature.

4 Using a serrated knife, slice the rings in half horizontally. Spread with cream cheese and replace the tops. Serve immediately.

1 teaspoon caraway seeds

1 teaspoon sesame seeds

1 teaspoon poppy seeds

1 teaspoon granulated onion

1 teaspoon granulated garlic

1 teaspoon flaky sea salt, such as Maldon brand

Pâte à Choux Dough (page 28)

1 large egg, lightly beaten

Cream cheese, softened, for serving

Note *Everything Bagels can also be "nothing bagels" by eliminating all the toppings. But where's the fun in that?*

Croque Monsieur Éclairs

MAKES 10 TO 12 LARGE ÉCLAIRS

1 Preheat the oven to 375°F. Line a baking sheet with aluminum foil.

2 Using a serrated knife, cut off the top one-third of each éclair shell lengthwise and discard. Spread 2 tablespoons of the béchamel sauce on the bottom of each éclair shell. Arrange the ham over the sauce.

3 Place the éclairs on the baking sheet. Sprinkle the ham generously with the cheese, season with pepper to taste, and bake for about 10 minutes, until the sandwiches are warm and the cheese has melted. Turn on the broiler, transfer the baking sheet to the broiler, and cook until the cheese has lightly browned, about 3 minutes. Serve immediately.

10 to 12 Large Éclair Shells (page 33)

Béchamel Sauce (page 256)

24 thin slices Virginia ham

½ cup (40 grams) grated Gruyère cheese

Ground black pepper, to taste

Note If you really want to get fancy, garnish your sandwiches with fried quail eggs and make your éclairs croque madames.

BÉCHAMEL SAUCE

1 In a medium saucepan, melt the butter over medium-low heat. Add the flour and whisk until smooth and dissolved. Continue to cook, while whisking constantly, until the mixture is light golden brown, about 3 minutes.

2 Slowly add the warm milk and salt, while whisking constantly until perfectly smooth. Cook until just thickened, about 7 minutes. Remove from the heat, add the cheese, nutmeg, and pepper to taste, and stir with a wooden spoon until well combined and the cheese has melted. Use while still warm, or refrigerate in an airtight container until ready to use, up to 2 days.

4 tablespoons (56 grams) unsalted butter

2 tablespoons (16 grams) unbleached all-purpose flour, sifted

1½ cups (360 grams) whole milk, warmed

½ teaspoon salt

2 cups (160 grams) grated Gruyère cheese

Pinch of ground nutmeg

Ground black pepper, to taste

Deviled Egg-clairs

1 Preheat the oven to 350°F. Line a baking sheet with parchment paper.

2 Fill a pastry bag fitted with a round piping tip (such as Ateco #806) with the pâte à choux dough. Pipe the dough by holding the tip at a 45-degree angle and squeezing the dough onto the baking sheet while slowly pulling the piping tip back to create an oval shape that is about the size of a large egg, leaving about 1 inch of space between each oval. Bake for 40 to 45 minutes, until deep golden brown and cooked through in the center. Let cool on the baking sheet to room temperature.

3 Using a serrated knife, cut the top one-third off of the oval shells and discard.

4 Fill a pastry bag fitted with a star piping tip (such as Ateco #825) with the deviled egg filling and pipe a rosette in the center of each egg éclair shell. Garnish with a pinch of paprika and a sprig of parsley, if desired. Serve immediately, or refrigerate for up to 8 hours.

Pâte à Choux Dough (page 28)

Deviled Egg Filling (page 258)

Paprika, for dusting (optional)

Sprigs of fresh flat-leaf parsley, for garnish (optional)

Note *If taking these on the road, pack the shells and filling separately, and fill on site just before serving.*

DEVILED EGG FILLING

Cut the eggs in half lengthwise. Remove the yolks and transfer to a large bowl. Add the mayonnaise, mustard, and vinegar to the yolks, and stir together until smooth and creamy. Season with salt and pepper to taste. Refrigerate until ready to use, up to 1 day.

Note *Don't throw those leftover hard-boiled egg whites in the trash! Serve them with chopped avocado, olive oil, salt, and a pinch of red pepper flakes for an incredibly delicious and healthy breakfast.*

12 large eggs, hard-boiled (see page 279) and peeled

½ cup (110 grams) mayonnaise

1 tablespoon (15 grams) Dijon mustard

2 teaspoons (10 grams) distilled white vinegar

Salt, to taste

Ground black pepper, to taste

Gruyère and Thyme Gougères

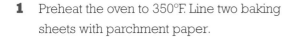

MAKES 30 TO 36 PIECES

1   Preheat the oven to 350°F. Line two baking sheets with parchment paper.

2   In a medium saucepan, bring the water, milk, butter, sugar, and salt to a rolling boil and cook until the butter has melted. Remove from the heat and add the flour all at once. Using a heat-resistant rubber spatula, stir the mixture until no lumps of dry flour remain, 1 to 2 minutes. Turn the heat to medium and cook the dough, while stirring constantly, until it forms a ball and leaves a skin on the base of the pot, 3 to 4 minutes. (If using a nonstick pan, a skin may not form on the base of the pot. Simply set a timer for 4 minutes instead.)

3   Transfer the dough to a large bowl and add 3 of the eggs, one at a time, stirring vigorously until the mixture is smooth between each addition. Scrape down the sides of the bowl with the rubber spatula as needed between each addition. Stir in the cheese, thyme, and pepper.

⅓ cup (80 grams) water

⅓ cup (80 grams) whole milk

5 tablespoons (70 grams) unsalted butter, cut into small pieces

1 teaspoon sugar

¼ teaspoon salt

¾ cup (105 grams) bread flour, sifted

4 large eggs

1¼ cups (100 grams) grated Gruyère cheese, plus more for topping

2 teaspoons (2 grams) fresh thyme leaves

Ground black pepper, to taste

Once the dough is fully combined, let it stand until it reaches room temperature, about 10 minutes.

4 Fill a pastry bag fitted with a round piping tip (such as Ateco #806) with the dough and pipe small mounds, about 1¼ inches in diameter and 1 inch tall, onto the baking sheets, leaving about 1 inch of space between each mound.

5 In a small bowl, lightly beat the remaining egg and then brush the tops of the mounds with the egg wash. Sprinkle each with a small pinch of grated cheese. Bake for 35 to 40 minutes, until deep golden brown and cooked through in the center. Serve warm, or let cool on the baking sheets to room temperature and store in an airtight container for up to 2 days.

Note *Gougères can be flavored with any combination of hard or semihard cheeses and fresh herbs, so use whatever you have on hand!*

Cheddar, Chipotle, and Roasted Corn Gougères

MAKES 30 TO 36 GOUGÈRES

1 In a small sauté pan, cook the corn in the olive oil over medium heat until the kernels are mostly light golden brown, about 5 minutes. Transfer the corn to a small bowl and let cool to room temperature.

2 Preheat the oven to 350°F. Line two baking sheets with parchment paper.

3 In a medium saucepan, bring the water, milk, butter, sugar, and salt to a rolling boil and cook until the butter has melted. Remove from the heat and add the flour all at once. Using a heat-resistant rubber spatula, stir the mixture until no lumps of dry flour remain, 1 to 2 minutes. Turn the heat to medium and cook the dough, while stirring constantly, until it forms a ball and leaves a skin on the base of the pot, 3 to 4 minutes. (If using a nonstick pan, a skin may not form on the base of the pot. Simply set a timer for 4 minutes instead.)

½ cup (75 grams) fresh corn kernels, cut from the cob

1 teaspoon olive oil

⅓ cup (80 grams) water

⅓ cup (80 grams) whole milk

5 tablespoons (70 grams) unsalted butter, cut into small pieces

1 teaspoon sugar

¼ teaspoon salt

¾ cup (105 grams) bread flour, sifted

4 large eggs

¾ cup (90 grams) shredded sharp cheddar cheese, plus more for topping

½ teaspoon ground chipotle chile pepper

4 Transfer the dough to a large bowl and add 3 of the eggs, one at a time, stirring vigorously until the mixture is smooth between each addition. Scrape down the sides of the bowl with the rubber spatula as needed between each addition of eggs. Stir in the cheese, corn, and chipotle chile pepper. Once the dough is fully combined, let it stand until it reaches room temperature, about 10 minutes.

5 Fill a pastry bag fitted with a round piping tip (such as Ateco #806) with the dough and pipe small mounds, about 1¼ inches in diameter and 1 inch tall, onto the baking sheets, leaving about 1 inch of space between each mound.

6 In a small bowl, lightly beat the remaining egg and then brush the tops of the mounds with the egg wash. Sprinkle each with a small pinch of cheese. Bake for 35 to 40 minutes, until deep golden brown and cooked through in the center. Serve warm, or let cool on the baking sheets to room temperature and then store in an airtight container for up to 2 days.

Note If you have cayenne pepper on hand, you can easily substitute ¼ teaspoon of that for the chipotle chile pepper.

BLT Sandwiches

MAKES 14 TO 16 SANDWICHES

Using a serrated knife, cut the cream puff shells in half horizontally. Spread the cut sides of each top and bottom with mayonnaise. Evenly divide the bacon, tomato, and lettuce among the bases of the cream puff shells, then place the tops over the lettuce. Serve the sandwiches immediately.

14 to 16 Large Cream Puff Shells (page 35)

½ cup (110 grams) mayonnaise

16 slices (16 ounces/453 grams) bacon, cooked and cut in half

2 ripe vine tomatoes, thinly sliced

8 large leaves Bibb lettuce, torn

▼ *Italian Muffuletta Sandwiches (page 266) and BLT Sandwiches*

Italian Muffuletta Sandwiches

Using a serrated knife, cut the cream puff shells in half horizontally, setting the tops next to their corresponding bottoms. Spread the cut sides of each top and bottom with about 1 tablespoon of the olive salad per side. Layer 1 slice each of the mozzarella, capicola, salami, mortadella, pepperoni, and provolone on the bottom of each cream puff shell. Set the tops of the cream puff shells over the provolone to sandwich together. Serve immediately, or refrigerate for up to 2 hours.

14 to 16 Large Cream Puff Shells (page 35)

Olive Salad (page 267)

14 to 16 slices shaved mozzarella cheese

14 to 16 slices shaved capicola or other cured Italian ham

14 to 16 slices shaved Genoa salami

14 to 16 slices shaved mortadella

14 to 16 slices shaved pepperoni

14 to 16 slices shaved provolone cheese

OLIVE SALAD

Stir all the ingredients together, transfer to an airtight container, and marinate in the refrigerator for at least 1 hour, or up to 1 week.

Note *I highly recommend you make a double batch of the olive salad, because you will want to eat it by the spoonful.*

1 cup (115 grams) mild or hot Italian giardiniera relish, store-bought

½ cup (85 grams) pimento-stuffed green olives, finely chopped

¼ cup (42 grams) Kalamata olives, pitted and finely chopped

2 tablespoons (20 grams) extra-virgin olive oil

2 tablespoons (20 grams) canola oil

1 tablespoon (15 grams) red wine vinegar

2 teaspoons (2 grams) dried oregano

1 teaspoon dried parsley

Salt, to taste

Ground black pepper, to taste

Parmesan-Prosciutto Sticks

◇ **MAKES ABOUT 30 STICKS** ◇

1 Preheat the oven to 350°F. Line two baking sheets with parchment paper.

2 In a medium saucepan, bring the water, milk, butter, sugar, and salt to a rolling boil and cook until the butter has melted. Remove from the heat and add the flour all at once. Using a heat-resistant rubber spatula, stir the mixture until no lumps of dry flour remain, 1 to 2 minutes. Turn the heat to medium and cook the dough, while stirring constantly, until it forms a ball and leaves a skin on the base of the pot, 3 to 4 minutes. (If using a nonstick pan, a skin may not form on the base of the pot. Simply set a timer for 4 minutes instead.)

3 Transfer the dough to a large bowl and add the eggs, one at a time, stirring vigorously until the mixture is smooth between each addition. Scrape down the sides of the bowl with the rubber spatula as needed between each addition. Stir in the cheese. Once the dough

⅓ cup (80 grams) water

⅓ cup (80 grams) whole milk

5 tablespoons (70 grams) unsalted butter, cut into small pieces

1 teaspoon sugar

¼ teaspoon salt

¾ cup (105 grams) bread flour, sifted

3 large eggs

⅔ cup (75 grams) grated Parmesan cheese

30 thin slices (450 grams) prosciutto

is fully combined, let it stand until it reaches room temperature, about 10 minutes.

4 Fill a pastry bag fitted with a round piping tip (such as Ateco #803) with the pâte à choux dough and pipe straight lines, about 8 inches long and ¼ inch wide, onto the baking sheets, leaving about ½ inch of space between each. Lightly moisten a fingertip with cold water and gently smooth any peaks or points created when piping. Bake for 30 to 35 minutes, until deep golden brown. Let cool on the baking sheets to room temperature.

5 Wrap a slice of prosciutto around the tip of each Parmesan stick and serve immediately.

Aged Gouda and Bacon Gougères

<o| **MAKES 30 TO 36 GOUGÈRES** |o>

1 Preheat the oven to 350°F. Line two baking sheets with parchment paper.

2 In a medium saucepan, bring the water, milk, butter, sugar, and salt to a rolling boil and cook until the butter has melted. Remove from the heat and add the flour all at once. Using a heat-resistant rubber spatula, stir the mixture until no lumps of dry flour remain, 1 to 2 minutes. Turn the heat to medium and cook the dough, while stirring constantly, until it forms a ball and leaves a skin on the base of the pot, 3 to 4 minutes. (If using a nonstick pan, a skin may not form on the base of the pot. Simply set a timer for 4 minutes instead.)

3 Transfer the dough to a large bowl and add 3 of the eggs, one at a time, stirring vigorously until the mixture is smooth between each addition. Scrape down the sides of the bowl with the rubber spatula as needed between

⅓ cup (80 grams) water

⅓ cup (80 grams) whole milk

5 tablespoons (70 grams) unsalted butter, cut into small pieces

1 teaspoon sugar

¼ teaspoon salt

¾ cup (105 grams) bread flour, sifted

4 large eggs

¾ cup (75 grams) grated aged Gouda cheese, plus more for topping

6 slices (6 ounces/170 grams) bacon, cooked and crumbled

Ground black pepper, to taste

each addition. Stir in the cheese, bacon, and pepper to taste. Once the dough is fully combined, let it stand until it reaches room temperature, about 10 minutes.

4   Fill a pastry bag fitted with a round piping tip (such as Ateco #806) with the dough and pipe small mounds, about 1¼ inch in diameter and 1 inch tall, onto the baking sheets, leaving about 1 inch of space between each mound.

5   In a small bowl, lightly beat the remaining egg and brush the tops of the mounds with the egg wash. Sprinkle each with a small pinch of cheese. Bake for 35 to 40 minutes, until deep golden brown and cooked through in the center. Serve warm, or let cool on the baking sheets to room temperature and then store in an airtight container for up to 2 days.

Note *Freeze an extra batch of your baked gougères for a last-minute dinner party hors d'oeuvre. Just place them in a 350°F oven for about 12 minutes to thaw and crisp up again before serving.*

New England Lobster Rolls

MAKES 10 TO 12 LOBSTER ROLLS

1 In a very large pot of boiling salted water, cook the lobsters until they turn bright red, 8 to 10 minutes. Using tongs, remove the lobsters from the boiling water and submerge in an ice water bath to stop the cooking, about 3 minutes. Remove the lobsters from the ice water bath, drain, and let cool to room temperature, about 20 minutes.

2 Separate the lobster tails and claws from the bodies of the lobsters and discard the bodies. Remove the meat from the tails and claws and chop the lobster meat into ¼-inch pieces. Transfer the chopped lobster meat to a strainer set over a bowl and refrigerate until very cold, at least 1 hour. (To cook raw lobster meat: Drain the juice from the meat. Over medium heat, bring 4 cups water and 4 tablespoons butter to a boil. Reduce the heat to a simmer. Place the meat in the simmering water and let cook for 4 to 6 minutes, or until firm. Drain the meat into a fine-mesh strainer and run under

4 (1- to 1¼-pound) Maine lobsters, or about 1 pound lobster meat, or 1 pound (454 grams) cooked lobster meat

¼ cup (55 grams) mayonnaise

¼ cup (30 grams) finely chopped celery, celery leaves reserved for garnish

2 tablespoons (28 grams) freshly squeezed lemon juice

2 pinches cayenne pepper

Salt, to taste

Ground black pepper, to taste

10 to 12 Large Éclair Shells (page 33)

1 stick (112 grams) unsalted butter, melted

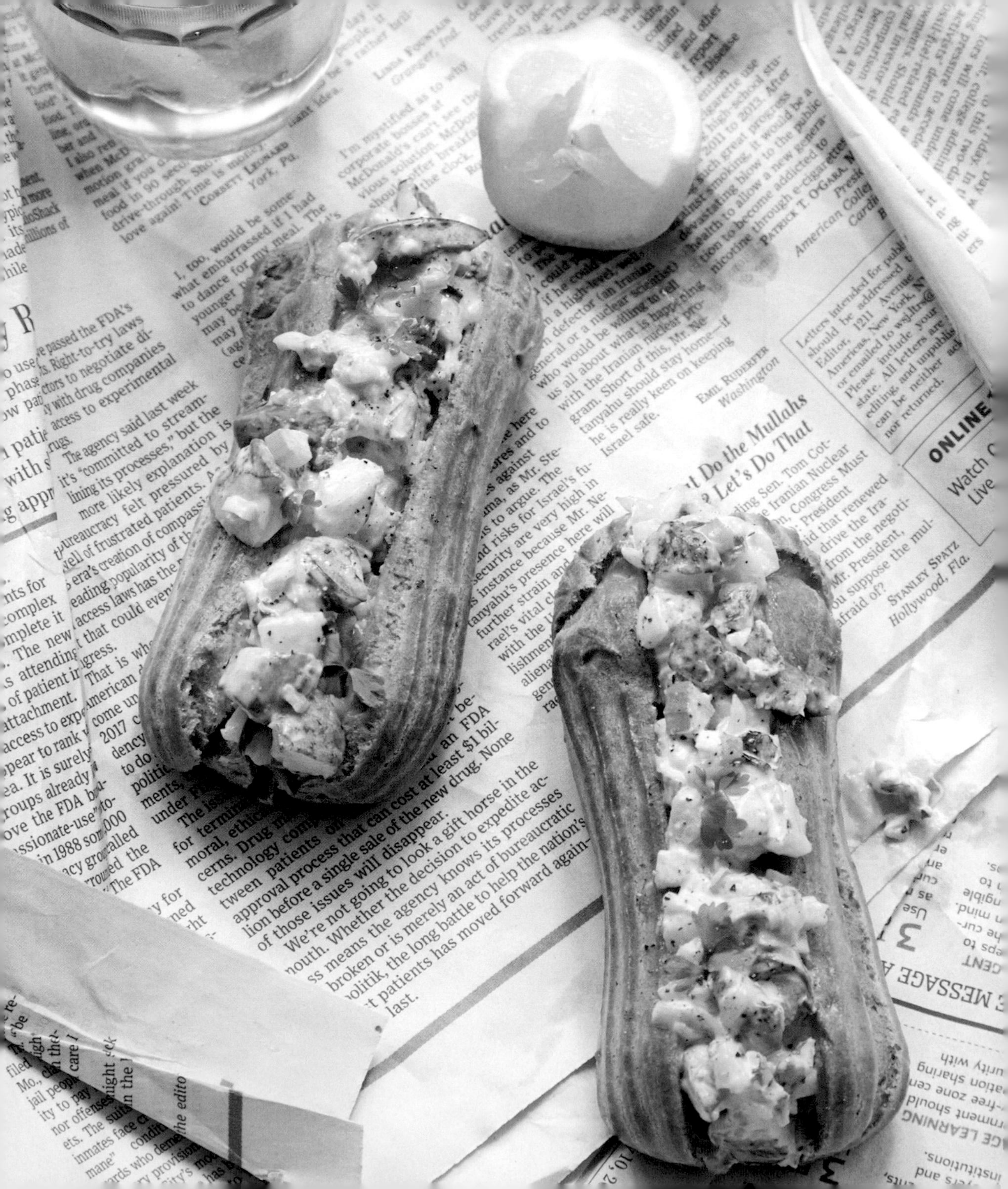

cold water until cooled to room temperature. Refrigerate the cooked lobster meat until very cold, at least 1 hour.)

3 In a large bowl, stir the chilled lobster meat with the mayonnaise, celery, lemon juice, cayenne, salt, and black pepper until well combined.

4 Using a serrated knife, split the éclair shells down the center like a hot dog bun. Brush the insides of each éclair shell with the melted butter. Fill each éclair shell with the lobster salad, garnish with the reserved celery leaves, and serve immediately.

Note *You can use éclair shells as an alternative for buns on any recipe you like to make. For example, they also make fun hot dog buns.*

Caprese Éclairs

Using a serrated knife, cut off the top one-third of each éclair lengthwise and discard. Spread a few teaspoons of the pesto in the bottom of each éclair shell. Arrange the mozzarella, tomatoes, and basil on top. Drizzle lightly with olive oil and season with salt and pepper to taste. Serve immediately.

Note To make this éclair a bit more gourmet, substitute burrata, an extra-creamy style of fresh mozzarella, for the bocconcini.

10 to 12 Large Éclair Shells (page 33)

¾ cup (200 grams) store-bought or homemade pesto sauce

1½ to 2 cups (225 to 300 grams) heirloom cherry tomatoes, halved or quartered

1½ to 2 cups (250 to 325 grams) bocconcini (small fresh mozzarella balls)

Leaves from 8 sprigs fresh basil

Extra-virgin olive oil, for drizzling

Salt, to taste

Ground black pepper, to taste

Egg Salad Éclairs

Using a serrated knife, cut off and discard the top one-third of the eclair shells. Spoon the egg salad into the shells and garnish with watercress leaves. Sprinkle with a pinch of salt and pepper and serve immediately.

10 to 12 Large Éclair Shells (page 33)

Egg Salad (recipe follows)

1 bunch watercress

Coarse sea salt, for sprinkling

Ground black pepper, for sprinkling

EGG SALAD

MAKES ABOUT 3 CUPS

Finely chop the eggs and place in a large bowl. Add the mayonnaise, onion, relish, and mustard, and stir together until well combined and smooth. Season with salt and pepper to taste. Refrigerate until ready to use, up to 2 days.

12 large eggs, hard-boiled and peeled

½ cup (110 grams) mayonnaise

¼ cup (35 grams) minced sweet onion

¼ cup (55 grams) sweet pickle relish

1 tablespoon (15 grams) Dijon mustard

Salt, to taste

Ground black pepper, to taste

Note To perfectly hard-boil large eggs, place the eggs in a large pot and fill with cold water to cover by about 1 inch. Over medium heat, bring the water to a boil. Cover the pot and remove from the heat. Let stand for exactly 12 minutes. Be sure to set a timer. Drain the eggs in a colander and place under cold running water to stop them from cooking. Peel as soon as they are cool enough to handle to prevent the shells from being difficult to remove.

Pâte à Choux Pizzelles

1 Preheat a pizzelle iron according to the manufacturer's instructions.

2 Lightly coat the iron with nonstick cooking spray and spoon about 1½ tablespoons of the pâte à choux dough onto to the center of the pizzelle press. Cook the pizzelles until the steam from the dough stops escaping from the sides of the press, about 1½ minutes. Repeat with the remainder of the dough. Serve immediately, or store in an airtight container for up to 3 days.

Nonstick cooking spray

Pâte à Choux Dough (page 28)

Note *Since these pâte à choux pizzelles, also used for ice cream sandwiches on page 200, aren't sweet, they make an excellent cracker to serve alongside savory spreads or a cheese platter.*

Acknowledgments

To the many, many hands that helped me bake up this cookbook:

I am especially grateful for my agent, Vicky Bijur. Thank you for being the first to recognize the potential of my pâte à choux project.

To my editor, Stephanie Fletcher: I am so appreciative for your immense faith in my abilities as a pastry chef and author. You gave me the freedom to write this book as creatively as I envisioned it.

To my photographer, Pernille Loof; my prop stylist, Brian Heiser; and my food stylist, Junita Bognanni—thank you for making my desserts look even better than I could make them. I missed you from all the way over on the other side of the room.

To graphic designer Rachel Newborn: Your masterful and magnificently whimsical designs captured my recipes and my voice just perfectly. Thank you for making this book totally adorable and approachable.

Thank you to those who tested every recipe, sometimes *over and over and over again*: Joanne Allegra, Carly Defilippo, Maia Baff, and Nevia Giles. Your hard work, detailed notes, feedback, and sometimes unwanted opinions helped shape my ideas into recipes that I am proud to share.

To Christina Tosi, thank you for your support and enthusiasm in this project. A lot of Milk Bar coffee and Compost Cookies got me through the writing of my manuscript.

Many thanks to the Institute of Culinary Education, especially Andrea Tutunjian, Director of Education and the Dean of the School of Pastry & Baking Arts, for being in full support of this cookbook, as well as a great employer. Your collaboration and facilities allowed me to execute this endeavor with ease.

A million and one thanks to the amazing cake designer, Kate Sullivan of Cake Power in NYC, and her lovely family, David, Sam, and CJ. I am so grateful for your generosity—letting my team take over your home and lives for a week of photos and great fun, and making the decorations for the Day of the Dead Éclairs (page 227).

All the cooks in the kitchen, I thank you for your efforts in helping me bake hundreds of desserts for the photos in the book: Eve Bergazyn, Jacqueline Evertsz, Dawn Kinard, Catherine Liu, Sandra Palmer, Christina Pagan, Camilla Tinoco, BéAnne Vivas, and Keren Weiner.

To my dear friend and pastry chef, Sandra Palmer, thank you. I could not have completed this book without you cheering me along the whole way.

To my friends and family: Sorry I didn't share more leftover éclairs from my recipe testing. I owe each one of you a batch of cream puffs.

SPECIAL THANKS

A very generous thanks to the Institute of Culinary Education, ABC Carpet and Home, Chef Rubber, Guittard, Le Creuset, Microplane, Vitamix, and Wüsthof for supplying bakeware, cookware, tableware, countertop appliances, tools, knives, chocolate, specialty ingredients, and decorations used for the recipe testing and photographs in this book.

Retail Therapy

INGREDIENTS

American Almond Products
718.875.8310
americanalmond.com

**Coombs Family Farms
Maple Syrup**
888.266.6271
coombsfamilyfarms.com

Goya
201.348.4900
goya.com/English

Guittard Chocolate Co.
800.HOT.CHOC
guittard.com

King Arthur Flour
802.649.3361
kingarthurflour.com

**Nellie and Joe's Famous
Key West Lime Juice**
800.LIME.PIE
keylimejuice.com

Nielsen-Massey
800.525.PURE
nielsenmassey.com

Odense Almond Paste
800.243.0897
odense.com

Singing Dog Vanilla
888.343.0002
singingdogvanilla.com

The Spice House
847.328.3711
thespicehouse.com

TOOLS AND SUPPLIES

ABC Carpet & Home
646.602.3101
abchome.com

All-Clad
800.255.2523
all-clad.com

Ateco
516.676.7100
atecousa.com

Chef Rubber
702.614.9350
chefrubber.com

Crate and Barrel
800.967.6696
crateandbarrel.com

Cuisinart
800.211.9604
cuisinart.com

Fishs Eddy
862.772.3971
fishseddy.com

KitchenAid
800.541.6390
kitchenaid.com

Le Creuset of America
877.418.5547
lecreuset.com

Microplane
800.555.2767
us.microplane.com

N.Y. Cake
212.675.CAKE
nycake.com

Williams-Sonoma
877.812.6235
williams-sonoma.com

Wüsthof
800.289.9878
wusthof.com

Index